HANDICAPPED INFANTS
AND CHILDREN

HANDICAPPED INFANTS AND CHILDREN

A Handbook for Parents and Professionals

Carol Tingey-Michaelis, Ph.D.
Associate Professor
Department of Psychology
Utah State University
Logan, Utah

University Park Press
Baltimore

UNIVERSITY PARK PRESS
International Publishers in Medicine and Human Services
300 North Charles Street
Baltimore, Maryland 21201

Typeset by The Oberlin Printing Company
Manufactured in the United States of America by The Maple Press Company

Photographs in figures 1, 2, 4-7, 10-15, 17-20, 22-24 by Sandstream, P.O. Box 28, Rockton, IL.

Library of Congress Cataloging in Publication Data

Tingey-Michaelis, Carol.
Handicapped infants and children.
Includes index.
1. Handicapped children—Care and treatment. I. Title.
RJ138.T55 1983 649'.151 83-6876
ISBN 0-8391-1771-X

CONTENTS

FOREWORD

Dr. Tingey-Michaelis' book is about long-term, home care of handicapped children. It is unique in its approach. The author outlines problem areas that parents are likely to meet in everyday life when raising their handicapped child at home. She discusses these problems in a straightforward, easily understood, and caring way. Not only does she provide direct and practical information for the here-and-now, but she also alerts parents to those circumstances that require professional or physician assistance. Both acute and chronic health and daily management problems are reviewed.

To help parents meet the needs of interdisciplinary program developers for their children, the book provides an outline of commonly required information. Background medical history, records of illnesses, immunizations, feeding habits, allergies, chronic medications, and details of seizure activity, if such occurs, are arranged in a way that is immediately useful to the child's evaluating physician. If parents would complete these as a permanent record, updated as needed, they would avoid much duplication and frustration.

In short, Dr. Tingey-Michaelis has compiled a book that fills a major void for every parent of handicapped children. Physicians and other health care providers will find the outline of problem areas, recommendations, and general guidance approach useful in their own practice. The author told me that she wanted to have the book as practical and informative as Dr. Spock's book has been for parents of normally developing children. I think she more than achieved her goal. In many ways the succinctness of discussion and unique lay-out may make it a much more valuable guide and "ready-reference" for parents than most such books.

The empathetic understanding reflected throughout this book comes from a person whose background is unusually suited to concerns for handicapped persons. She is a university professor in educational psychology, with her doctorate in developmental psycholinguistics. Additional postdoctoral work in occupational and physical therapy, and teacher-trainer experience in special education training programs have rounded her background with the general knowledge needed for this undertaking. Although her interest and educational direction have been toward benefitting handicapped persons from the outset, they were amplified by the birth and subsequent needs of her own handicapped son, Jim, born with Down syndrome. Raising Jim, his three brothers, and sister to be effective and contributing adults is a major lifetime accomplishment in itself. Her doctoral work and subsequent university activities followed rearing her family. This work is a beginning for her, rather than a culmination. She is certain to provide meaningful professional input for her colleagues and for parents of the children she loves for many years to come.

Dr. Tingey-Michaelis' personal contribution to the literature for home management of handicapped persons is, above all, the concern and understanding she expresses for their parents, and for the anxieties and frustrations they meet in day-to-day living circumstances. So often parents need emotional support when the burdens of their child's care seem excessive, and they also need accurate and meaningful information about their child's needs. This book provides that kind of parent "back-up." I am honored to be asked to review the book and to write its foreword.

I know that the persons who use this book—parents, physicians, other health care providers, educators, social workers, and psychologists involved with care of the handicapped—will find it a worthwhile and valuable text for their home or office. They, as I have, will read and incorporate its concepts almost automatically, and will find themselves referring clientele to it for guidance.

Jack A. Madsen, M.D.
Professor, Departments of Neurology and Pediatrics
School of Medicine
University of Utah
Salt Lake City, Utah
Director of Neurological Services
Utah State Training School
American Fork, Utah

PREFACE

IF YOU HAVE A SPECIAL CHILD, YOU WILL PROBABLY WORRY MORE THAN OTHER PARENTS

You may have these worries about yourself:

Does my child have problems because of something I did?

Does he have problems because of something I didn't do?

Is there something that I can do, or can I find someone to do something that will cure the problems?

How am I going to take care of this baby and do all the other things that I'm supposed to do or that I want to do?

If I have another baby will that baby have problems, too?

You may worry about the baby:

What will my child be like when he grows up?

How will I take care of him?

It is natural to worry about these things.

Other parents of special babies are worrying, too;

in fact

all parents worry some

FINDING THE ANSWERS

Many of the things that parents of special children worry about don't really have answers.

There are some things that your special baby will need that no one really knows yet.

Sometimes it is necessary to keep trying things until something works, but when you are tired of trying you must rest for a while.

THOSE WHO CAN HELP

Doctors know how to help you learn what to do to make your baby healthy.

Special teachers have been trained to help you know how you can let your child's mind grow.

Nurses have been trained to help you learn how to care for your baby's body.

Therapists have been trained to help you learn how to help your baby learn to move and how to talk.

NONE OF THEM KNOWS ALL THE ANSWERS
BUT TOGETHER THEY CAN HELP YOU
FIND SOME OF THE ANSWERS

YOU CAN HELP THE MOST

You can do more for your child than anyone else because you will be with him more than anyone else.

You will know him better than anyone else does.

Your baby will grow and learn from the little things that happen day after day.

You will be the one making decisions about the little things that will be happening.

MAKING DECISIONS

It is hard to know when your special child needs special consideration and when he needs to do the things that other babies are doing.

SOMETIMES, BECAUSE THEY HAVE BEEN TRAINED IN DIFFERENT WAYS,

one professional may tell you to do one thing,

another professional may tell you to do another thing.

*AND the grandparents will tell you
to do it yet a different way.*

IT IS SOMETIMES HARD TO KNOW WHOSE ADVICE TO TAKE.

You *must be the one who decides which of the people giving advice has had the most experience with special children and what you will do.*

The more comfortable you become with the day-to-day decisions, the less you will worry.

THIS BOOK IS WRITTEN TO HELP YOU MAKE THOSE DECISIONS.

DECIDE TO TAKE A BREAK NOW AND THEN

Although you probably will not want someone else making the decisions for you,

Sometimes it would be good to have someone else take care of your baby so you can get some rest;

*or take care of your other children,
or get some work done,
or just do something fun!*

WORRYING ABOUT YOUR BABY ALL THE TIME IS NOT GOOD FOR HIM OR FOR YOU.

Find someone who has had experience with babies and tell her your baby's schedule. Have her visit you and your baby and show her where the baby's things are. Then trust her to make the little decisions for awhile.

While you are away, try to forget about your child for awhile and enjoy yourself.

WHEN YOU ARE AWAY FROM YOUR BABY NOW AND THEN, YOU WILL BE BETTER ABLE TO CARE FOR HIM WHEN YOU ARE WITH YOUR BABY . . .

HOW TO HELP YOUR CHILD MAINTAIN GOOD HEALTH

Having good health means being free from disease and pain. A healthy person is able to enjoy more things than one who is not well. This is true not only for your child, but for you . . .

Be sure to get enough rest, food, and exercise; then you can enjoy holding, talking to, and taking care of your baby.

You can't protect your child's health unless you protect your own . . .

TO KEEP YOUR BABY HEALTHY YOU WILL NEED TO

1. Take him to your pediatrician or family doctor for regular visits.
2. Be careful with his diet, watch his weight, and give him vitamins just like other babies.
3. See that he gets immunizations and booster shots just as all babies do.
4. Learn what he needs and how to meet those needs, then be comfortable and relaxed while taking care of the baby, as if he were just like other babies.

CAREFUL CHOICE OF A PEDIATRICIAN OR FAMILY DOCTOR *is more important if you have a special baby*

Some doctors care more than others about the problems that special babies have.

Choose a doctor who seems to be comfortable with your child and with whom you are comfortable. Ask other mothers about their doctors. Ask the doctor if he or she wants a special baby as a patient.

If the doctor is to be helpful to you, he must know you and your child well and be interested in your progress.

ROUTINE VISITS TO THE DOCTOR CAN BE EXHAUSTING

It is not just the organization of the house and getting there that is difficult;
    you must also remember the things that you have been concerned about so you can talk to the doctor about them.

You might want to keep a notebook just for notes about the baby.

You could write questions when you think of them, then take the notebook to the doctor's office so you can remember your questions.

You could write the answers in the notebook as the doctor gives them to you, or record his answers on a cassette.

Even when your questions have been answered during the visit, it is hard to remember later exactly what the doctor said unless you have a record.

TAKING THE BABY TO A SPECIALIST IS A TRYING EXPERIENCE,

Of course you want to know all there is about your child's problem but it makes you remember your sad feelings—or even makes you feel sadder.

Some parents go from one specialist to another, trying to find someone who can really help the baby.

Although it is wise to get all the help you can, competent specialists trade information and one specialist is not likely to know more than another.

Since taking the child to a specialist is such a trying experience, it would be wise to plan to set aside other stressful things and take it easy just before and just after the evaluation.

Although mother may be used to taking the child out alone, it is unwise for her to try to manage the trip to the specialist singlehanded.

If father is not able to go with the mother, then careful arrangements should be made for someone else whom the mother enjoys being with to accompany her.

This might be a grandparent or a friend. It is important that the person not be someone the mother must take care of, but someone who can provide support and comfort for the mother.

Take your notebook or cassette recorder along so you can ask and get answers to all your questions.

Although you will want to take the advice of the pediatrician, family doctor, or specialist, remember that the baby is *your* baby and the day-to-day decisions are yours.

HOW TO USE THIS BOOK

This book is organized like a dictionary or an encyclopedia. It is a list of problems that special babies and their parents have had. *No child has all of these problems.* And you will probably not want to read about all of them. *It would probably depress you.*

You may want to refer to an appropriate section when you are having a specific problem. The problems are listed under the general headings of: health, feeding, sleep, movement, social, language, self-help, and specific health problems and syndromes. In the list there are small problems that relate to larger problems. When a problem in one area is related to a problem in another there is a cross-reference note. If the exact problem that your child is having is not listed you might look through the list again to see if there is a problem similar to your child's. Sometimes knowing the solution to a similar problem can help you find a way to deal with your personal situation.

Being the parent of a child with special needs is very lonely at times. Some of those times you will need help but all anyone will be able to offer is sympathy. Maybe, after you cry a little, it will help to curl up with this book. It is full of what other parents and experienced professionals would tell you—if they were there.

I

You May Be Concerned About the Things That Could Disrupt Your Baby's Health

1 SOME CHILDREN HAVE SHORT SPELLS OF BLACKING OUT—IT IS SOMETIMES CALLED A CONVULSION OR A SEIZURE

Some babies blink their eyes and stare into space or do not seem to be looking at you though facing you. The body may go stiff or limp at the same time. Sometimes the arms and legs move a lot or jerk at the same time.

Many babies have some of these spells or convulsions. If your baby does it is important to know exactly what the child does at these times. Try to be calm and watch. Although it is frightening, babies do not usually hurt themselves or receive any permanent damage from a convulsion. If the child is walking, he may fall and bump his head, but the injury is from the fall, not from the convulsion. Since a spell or convulsion cannot be predicted, you will have to watch closely and then describe to the doctor or nurse what happens. It is a good idea to write down:

1. Exactly what the baby did: blink eyes, go stiff, one or both sides?
2. About how long it lasted: 10 seconds, 20 seconds—look at the clock!
3. What the baby did when it was over: sleep, scream, urinate, smile?
4. How often this happens: keep a record on the calendar, write the time of day.

Seizures which occur repeatedly can be epilepsy.

If a seizure causes the baby to go blue, lasts longer than 5 minutes, or recurs repeatedly in a period of time, call the doctor and tell the nurse that it is an emergency.

While some seizures occur infrequently, others can occur repeatedly—hundreds of times daily. Finding the cause of seizures can be very important, and attempts to do this should be made as soon as a seizure problem is recognized. Most will not have a specific cause that can be corrected, but some will. Others have to be treated by giving medicine daily. If given appropriately, drugs can prevent or control most seizure problems and can do so with very few side effects. Find a child neurologist, or neurologist or pediatrician in your area who has a *special interest* in epilepsy. They will be the doctors who can help you most (see page 180).

If the baby has a convulsion in connection with a fever or vomiting, there may be some illness that needs to be treated. However, if the baby is not sick from something else, you should not treat him as if he were. After a convulsion or a seizure he may be tired and want to rest. However, if the baby does not seem tired, it is best to continue doing what you were doing before the seizure.

A spell or convulsion is more likely to occur when the child is not getting the proper amount of rest, is hungry, or is emotionally upset. It is important to follow a regular feeding and sleeping schedule if the child has a seizure disorder.

2   SOME BABIES ROCK THEIR BODIES, HIT THEIR HEADS, OR CHEW ON THEMSELVES—IT IS SOMETIMES CALLED SELF-STIMULATION

If the child self-stimulates to the extent of bruising or injury it is called self-mutilation. This is usually possible to prevent if you learn to deal with self-stimulation.

It is important for you to know that although you are upset you should not feel guilty. Your child is not trying to punish you or make you feel guilty or make you feel that you are a bad parent. The baby is only doing what feels good to him.

You need not feel ashamed nor need to explain to your friends, or neighbors or even relatives, unless you feel that they are close to you and could be helpful.

Sometimes doctors or therapists suggest placing some covering over the child's hands or that something be put on the child's elbows so he can't get the hand to the face to hurt himself.

It is most important to get some help to find why the baby keeps bumping or hitting or scratching.

Moving makes the body feel good. Moving back and forth feels so good to some babies that they spend a lot of time rocking back and forth. Some also like the feeling of having their head hit against something so they move to a place where their head can hit against the side of the crib or a pillow or something firm while they rock their bodies.

Some infants hold their hand up against a bright light and watch while they move the hand. Some babies learn to like the feeling that comes from hitting their face or other parts of their body.
Some like the feeling they get when they rub their eyes so much that they hit at them or put their fingers into their own eyes.
Some babies like the feeling they get when they rub their sex organs.
Some infants like the feeling of sucking and chewing so much that they suck and chew whatever is close. Often this is the child's hand, which becomes sore when it is sucked and chewed all the time. Some cream or medicine can heal it, but you must find ways for the baby's mouth to get used to sucking and chewing something else. A therapist would call this oral desensitization or helping the mouth feel more normally. This is done by carefully applying firm pressure to the lips and inside of the mouth.

Babies make these repeated movements because they need *more movement* to feel the sensation. They need to be bounced on the knee, tossed in the air, held sideways. They need to have soft things and textured things touch their bodies. They need to play in water and sand. They need to learn finger plays and to eat with their hands. If your child has special problems it is easy to be overly protective. But protecting a child from being carried and being played with and getting dirty can prevent him from developing.

A physical therapist or an occupational therapist who works with babies can show you some ways to help your child get used to the feeling of moving in other ways. Then he will not need to keep repeating the same movement and can learn to enjoy some other movements.

By watching your baby's movement the therapist can design some things for you to do that will particularly help *your* baby.

If your child is already self-stimulating so much that there are bruises and bleeding, or bruises and sores, you may need the help of a teacher or a psychologist who can help you carefully organize the baby's life to modify (change) the behavior, in addition to the therapist to help you learn how to help the baby move his body.

Part of the reason that the baby self-stimulates may be because of some movement or central nervous system problems. Look at Motor Problems 4, 5, and 7 for more information about this.

Babies are more likely to start self-stimulation if they are left alone often (particularly in bed) and do not have toys or people around to touch them and talk to them.

So be sure you do the things the therapist has suggested especially for your baby and continue therapy to help you know what stimulation your baby needs next.

It may be that in order for you to have more time to play with your baby you will need someone to help with the housework or with the other children.

It may be helpful to get away from children and do something you enjoy with adults from time to time. Then, when you care for your special baby, you can enjoy him and not feel bored or isolated.

3 SOME BABIES HAVE DIGESTION AND ELIMINATION PROBLEMS

Many children have trouble because they have too loose or too firm bowel movements. The most effective way to treat this is through diet. Fruit juices tend to make the waste looser. Solid foods tend to make the waste more solid. Bran cereal adds bulk to the stools. The doctor or nurse can give you a specific list of foods that may help your baby.

Babies who are not able to move other parts of the body may have trouble moving the bowels, too. If the child learns to move the trunk of the body so the shoulders and hips can move separately, the organs of the digestive system will be able to function better. Regular exercise can help the bowels move. Sometimes suppositories or enema may be necessary.

A physical or occupational therapist can show you how to help the body move so the bowels will move more regularly.

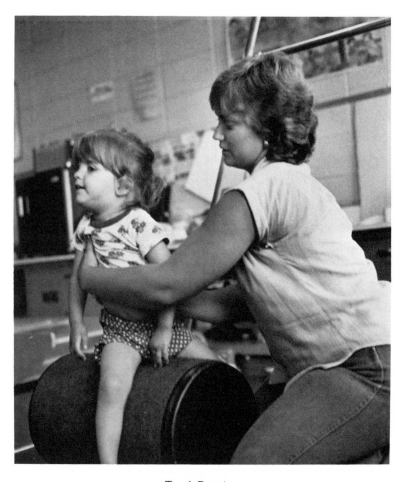

Trunk Rotation

Trunk Rotation

If the child is uncomfortable and is having trouble digesting unusual foods, the stomach may hurt and the baby may curl up in a ball and cry. It helps to make sure he is warm, even feet and hands. Sometimes it helps to rub his back or the tummy, if he will let you. It is most important to examine the foods that were eaten and consider the possible strain caused by illness or change in the usual routine.

SOME FOODS MAY BOTHER YOUR BABY

Hives and rash happen from time to time. Often they result from the foods that have been eaten. It is wise to feed new foods one at a time and to wait at least a week before feeding another new one. That way you will have a better idea if a certain food bothers your child. It may be convenient to keep this record on a calendar.

Sugar, salt and artificial color and flavoring are not good for babies. They can cause rash and they may aggravate a baby's restlessness and irritability.

The digestive process is closely related to how a person feels and babies react to the feelings of their parents. If parents are tense and anxious, it is possible for the baby to respond with upsets in the digestion/elimination process. Children who have frequent problems with digestion and elimination are likely to have parents who are very concerned and nervous. The parents usually have "nervous stomachs" themselves. If you have a nervous stomach you may want to learn to relax for the sake of both your and your baby's stomach, you may be interested in reading the book:

Gut Reaction: How to Handle Stress and Your Stomach by D. M. Taylor and M. A. Rock. The Saunders Press, Philadelphia, 1980.

4 BABIES SOMETIMES HAVE DIFFICULTY BREATHING

They might make wheezy sounds when they breathe or they might cough and choke frequently. Sometimes this is caused by respiratory problems and sometimes it is caused by an allergy or infection. Other times it is because the child feels upset and uncomfortable. It may take careful observation to learn what the cause is.

YOU CAN HELP MAKE THIS OBSERVATION BY CAREFULLY NOTICING WHEN THE BABY HAS TROUBLE BREATHING:

What is he doing at the time?
What kind of clothing is he wearing?
What kind of clothing are those near the baby wearing?
Is he close to pets or places where pets play?
What fabrics or materials are used in household furnishings?
What has he been eating?

If the climate is dry the child's breathing may improve if a vaporizer is used. There are many inexpensive models that use cold water and are quite safe to leave running all day or overnight. The moisture vaporized in the air helps the inside of the nose and the lungs. The moisture also helps prevent nosebleed.

If the child usually breathes well, but has sudden trouble breathing, check to see if he has a fever. Sometimes illness can cause breathing difficulty. If there is a fever and the baby is not breathing well, it is best to check with the doctor. A fever is the response of the body to fighting infection. For a baby it might be a slight infection or it may be something that is serious. Only the doctor can tell that.

Many babies with special problems have noses that seem to run all of the time. Sometimes this is because the child cannot feel when the nostril is full and sometimes it is full because the baby is having trouble learning how to blow air through his nose to clear it.

You may need to use a *syringe* to help keep the nostrils clean. Do this several times a day and night, especially at bedtime.

Keeping the baby on his stomach will help drain the nose and keep it clear. Nose drops or decongestants should only be used a few days at a time.

Your baby will be able to breathe easier if you are relaxed and calm.

When you are nervous and when you get excited because the child is having trouble breathing, the baby gets nervous, too. Breathing is more difficult when the body is tense. Parents who get excited about the breathing problems actually cause the problems to get worse.

5 SOME BABIES SEEM TO GET SICK EASILY

Some spit up after almost every meal and seem to have trouble with gas and cramps all the time. If your baby does be sure that:

1. You carefully burp the baby several times during the feeding. Some infants tend to breathe more through the mouth and they swallow air. When a baby cries there is more chance of swallowing air. Air trapped in the digestive tract is uncomfortable (see Feeding Problems, 1).
2. Do not allow anyone to bounce or move the child around quickly just after he has eaten.
3. Sit down, allow yourself plenty of time, and relax when you are feeding the baby. Talk to him. Sometimes it helps to have soothing music playing. If you have other children, it may be a good time for one of them to hold a book for you to read to them during feeding time.

> If you are tense when you hold the baby, he can feel it. Try to be calm and make feeding time as much as possible like a dinner party. The section about feeding problems has more information about babies who have trouble swallowing and learning to feed themselves.

SOME BABIES HAVE TROUBLE WITH THEIR NOSES.

> The child may pick at his nose or rub it, if there is dust that causes irritation.
>> Feathers, wool blankets, rugs and upholstery can cause irritation. So can pet hairs and household dust.
>>> If the nose itches and is continually rubbed or picked with the finger it is more likely to bleed.

Some babies have a lot of nosebleeds.

The nose is more likely to bleed when the air is dry (see vaporizer page 8).

The nose is more likely to bleed if mucous is allowed to dry on the outside and inside of the nose (see syringe page 9). Then the sensitive skin of the nose will be irritated when you try to clean it.

Children who live at high altitudes are likely to have trouble with nosebleeds. If nosebleeds happen more than once a week, check with your doctor to see if there may be some difficulty with blood clotting.

Children who bump their heads against the bed or pillow are more likely to have nosebleeds (see Health Problems, 2).

SOME BABIES HAVE FREQUENT FEVERS.

When the body is fighting infection the temperature rises. The temperature can rise very quickly and the baby will be uncomfortable.

If your child's temperature is more than 100° (F) as often as once a week it would be a good idea to have the doctor check the baby carefully.

Very high temperatures are not only uncomfortable for the child but they can cause permanent damage to the central nervous system. Sometimes the baby's temperature can be lowered by bathing, in water that is about room temperature. Dry the baby and keep him dressed in light clothing to avoid becoming chilled.

Although it is not uncommon for a child to have a fever from time to time, it may be a sign of other problems if the fever returns or if the baby runs a fever day after day.

It is not a good idea to guess your baby's temperature from just touching him. Your own hand could be cold or warm. Get a rectal thermometer, learn how to use it and read it. Check with your doctor before using aspirin. It can cause problems.

When your baby has a fever he will be fussy and irritable. Remember this is natural and try to keep from worrying.

ALL PARENTS WORRY WHEN THEIR BABIES ARE SICK.
BUT PARENTS OF SPECIAL BABIES WORRY MORE.

It is easy to think that the illness may be the beginning of more serious problems. Sometimes parents worry about whether the child will grow up to be strong.
It is also natural for the parents of special babies to worry about their child not ever getting well, even if he is just sick with a cold or some common childhood disease.

Be sure that you get plenty of rest and take little naps if you have been up in the night. You may need someone to help you with the other children and the housework. Try to force yourself to be calm and comfortable with the baby and expect him to get well.

Your baby will get well faster and stay well longer if you are calm and relaxed while caring for him.

If your doctor has given a prescription, use it as directed. A follow-up visit is important to be sure that the infection is gone.

When your child is exposed to a virus—and there are hundreds of them—he will catch a cold. This is a normal part of growing up and your child will "catch colds" while he is developing immunity to each of the viruses. When the child has a cold he will cough to clear the mucous from his throat. The cough may last for a week or so.

If the cough is severe and causes breathing problems, there could be complications in the lungs.
Infection in the lungs is called pneumonia.

If your baby has: high fever
severe cough
rapid breathing
and generally is uncomfortable and restless

have the doctor see him so the doctor can decide what is causing the infection and can prescribe the proper medication for your baby.

Then follow the doctor's advice about bed rest, liquids, and medication.

6   SOME BABIES GET TIRED VERY EASILY

BABIES WITH HEART PROBLEMS AND BABIES WITH MOVEMENT PROBLEMS
    WILL BECOME TIRED VERY EASILY

It is important for them to have regular rest periods during the day.

It is important to plan the day so the baby can rest comfortably.
    A good car bed and perhaps a bed at grandmother's or other places where you fre-
    quently visit would be helpful.

Try to be pleasant and matter of fact about the child's need to rest.
    Try to remember that from the baby's point of view, it is natural to need so much rest.

But be careful not to limit the child more than necessary.

BABIES LEARN BY BEING WITH OTHERS AND DOING THINGS

Even when the baby is resting, have some
        toys or pictures to play with. You can
        make an interesting picture book by
        putting pictures on cardboard and cov-
        ering them with clear contact paper.

                The pages could be used separately or made
                        into a book by punching holes in them
                        and fastening them with large metal
                        rings or lacing the pages together.

                                If you use pictures of the family members
                                        and pets the child can be learning even
                                        when resting.

SOME BABIES SEEM TO BE LISTLESS AND TIRED ALL OF THE TIME

*If your child does not coo and smile at you, it is easy for you to feel that he is not
    happy . . .
    . . . and maybe you are not a good parent.*

Some children do not have as much energy as others and do not move as quickly or try to
    reach for toys or climb on things as much as other babies.

Be sure to have your doctor check to see if the child has some infection. Be sure that you keep the baby healthy (see pages 1-20). Make sure that your baby has a regular routine of food, rest, and exercise.

Then don't worry about the health.
Keep the healthy daily routine.
Talk to your baby and play with him.
Show him interesting things.
Allow him to play with safe objects.

DON'T ALLOW THE BABY TO CRY UNTIL HE TURNS BLUE

If your child has heart problems, it does not take much crying for him to turn blue. Try not to show alarm, but attend to his needs quickly.
Sometimes babies hold their breath to tell you that they don't like certain foods or even to tell you that they are not comfortable.

IF YOUR CHILD SUDDENLY GOES BLUE WHILE YOU ARE HOLDING HIM, SHAKE HIM GENTLY AND CALL HIS NAME

If the baby turns blue and you cannot arouse him by shaking and calling his name then he needs *IMMEDIATE MOUTH-TO-MOUTH BREATHING:*

1. Clear the air passage. Put your finger into the baby's mouth and take out any food or object that may be there.

2. Help the baby start breathing by breathing in his mouth and nose. Cover the mouth and nose with your mouth. Breathe once into the mouth and nose then move away and repeat.

You may want to take a class to learn how to do mouth-to-mouth breathing. Call the local hospital or heart association. They have classes from time to time that you can join. You will feel more comfortable if you are sure that you know what to do in this emergency.

BABIES WHO DO NOT SEE WELL ARE NOT ABLE TO SMILE WHEN YOU SMILE AT THEM

They also do not try to crawl to get things and they do not reach for toys or move around to get them as much as other babies since they cannot see them.

It will help to give the baby a safe place to play near you and give him some toys that make noise.

It is also important to *talk* to your child about what you are doing and he is doing while the activity is happening.

Help your baby to *see* things by touching them and hearing them if they make noise.

BABIES WHO DO NOT HEAR WELL DO NOT COO TO THEMSELVES OR TRY TO COO BACK WHEN SOMEONE TALKS TO THEM

They are not attracted to go and see what is making the noise, since they do not hear it.

If the child does not hear household noises, he will not crawl to play with the radio, piano, or vacuum cleaner as much as other babies.

He may be able to hear only very loud noises and may like to sit and hold onto the washer or vacuum cleaner.

It is important that you talk to your baby and that you make sure he can see your face when you are talking. Then help him "hear" things by making sure he can see and touch things. Take him up close to the object or let him crawl close.

THE BABY MAY HEAR AND SEE BUT NOT HAVE SUFFICIENT ENERGY TO EXPLORE

If the child's heart has trouble keeping a steady rhythm or if the heart valve does not close tightly, there will not be enough oxygen in the blood and that will make the baby feel "tired."

Sometimes the problem can be corrected with surgery, but if your child has heart problems it is important to have your doctor explain what to look for so you will know when your baby is tired.

Exploring and trying things for themselves is the way babies learn. You will prevent learning if you don't encourage the child to do things for himself as much as possible.

Other problems may cause frequent "tiredness." Be sure that the baby's blood is normal, and that his metabolism is functioning well. Sometimes thyroid function is low, causing "tiredness." Sometimes diabetes can cause the tired feeling.

Some babies who have trouble learning have eyes, ears, and hearts that work fine.

BUT THEY ARE SLOW IN BEING ABLE TO LEARN FROM WHAT THEY SEE AND HEAR

They may be slow in wanting to move close
    enough to touch and play with things.

They may be slow in knowing when someone is talking to them and in knowing how to smile
    or coo back.

Your baby may not respond quickly, but keep showing and helping him touch things. Keep
    talking to your baby.

EVEN THOUGH HE DOES NOT SEEM TO BE ABLE TO UNDERSTAND

It will be necessary for some special babies to see and hear and touch many times before they
    understand enough to smile, touch, and want to move close to other people and things.

It just takes time.

FOR SOME BABIES IT WILL TAKE QUITE A LOT OF TIME

> But don't give up,
>   keep smiling, keep talking
>   and keep showing the baby all the little things
>   that happen day after day.

(See Language Problems)

7 SOME BABIES HAVE PROBLEMS WITH THEIR EYES

Some children wake up in the morning or from naps, with white or yellowish matter on the eyelids. Sometimes it is dried and the baby can't open his eyes.

He may cry or fuss. Gently wash around the eyes with a cotton ball and some warm water. Dry the area with another cotton ball.

All babies have this happen sometimes.

If it happens more than once a week, check with your doctor to see if there is an infection. It is likely to be an infection if the baby is fussy and has a fever, or if the eyes are swollen and red.

It could also be that the tear ducts are stopped up and not draining properly. The doctor may need to clear them or they may clear themselves in a day or two. If they don't clear themselves in two days the doctor may need to clear them for you.

The matter in the eyes could also be caused by an allergy. It is important to see if there are some things that may cause the allergy for the baby (see Health Problems, 4). An allergy or itching in the eyes can be the beginning of eye rubbing and putting fingers in the eyes (see Health Problems, 2).

FOR SOME PROBLEMS AN OPTHALMOLOGIST WHO HAS WORKED WITH CHILDREN NEEDS TO LOOK AT YOUR BABY.

Those problems are:

Extra sensitivity to sunlight. Although it is natural to blink and squint for a few minutes in bright sunlight, if this continues all the time outdoors, the baby may need some treatment.

If the black center or pupil of the eyes seem to be cloudy or milky, it might mean that the lens of the eye has become so thick that it is difficult to see through the eye. The cloudy lens is called a cataract. We usually think of people having cataracts when they get old, but sometimes babies are born with them. It is usually possible to surgically remove a cataract.

If the eyes move or jerk slightly all of the time, it is possible to see, but you need to know if there is some treatment that will help the baby see better.

If the eyes do not focus together, it is hard for the brain to make the two pictures into one picture. The picture from the strong eye becomes more important and the weak eye gets weaker and weaker until sometimes it won't see any more. Early surgery can sometimes straighten the muscle in the weaker eye. Or a patch over the good eye can help the weak eye be used more and therefore develop more. Sometimes you will be told that the baby will outgrow this problem, but don't accept this answer. You need the help of an opthalmologist who has had experience with children.

After a child is one year of age the vision acuity can be checked. With special tests it can be done even earlier. Poor eyesight can often be corrected with glasses. Most children accept glasses if they really need them to see clearly.

8 SOME BABIES HAVE EAR PROBLEMS

If your baby has fluid draining out of the ear that is yellowish white or brownish white, it is important to have the doctor examine him. It is possible that there is an infection in the inner ear even though the child has not complained or been fussy.

There might also be infection, even if there are no fluids draining out of the ear. There is a small tube that goes from the nose and throat to the inner ear. Since the tubes are short and straight in babies, it is easy for infection from colds or other breathing problems to travel quickly to the ear drum area.

If the baby is holding the ears and crying or hitting and scratching the ears, there also might be infection.

Ear infections need *Immediate* treatment to prevent the infection from damaging the inner ear. Sometimes babies who began to hit or scratch the ear repeatedly because of an infection may continue (see Health Problems, 2).

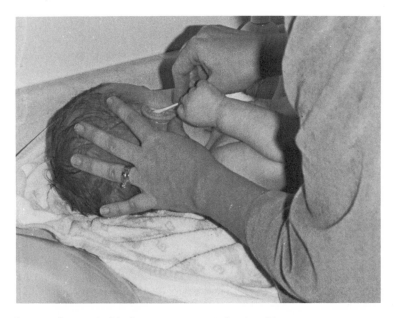

Protecting the ears from wind helps prevent ear infection. You may want to put cotton in the ears on cold (or even warm) windy days. Be sure that the bed or play area is not in a place where a fan or heat register blows. Riding in a car with an open window may cause ear troubles. Whenever the baby may be exposed to moving air it is wise to put a light weight cap that covers the ears on him.

If he cries or puts hands over ears when there are loud noises it may be wise to have the hearing checked.

If he does not look at you and smile when you call the baby by name or coo and make noises when playing, he may have a hearing problem. You will be able to help your baby learn even though the baby cannot hear if you learn special ways to interact with the baby (see Language Problems). Ask your doctor about a specialist who can test hearing. Then be sure that you find a specially trained teacher to help you learn how to work and play with your baby.

9 OTHER HEALTH CONCERNS THAT YOU MIGHT HAVE

Babies drool, spit up, and spill, but usually only when they are eating. If your baby does it at other times you may want to have enough bibs to keep a clean one on all the time. Or you may want to have plenty of tee shirts and change them frequently. Having the chest damp all the time is not healthy.

Sometimes babies who have central nervous system problems do not learn to swallow automatically and the saliva drips from the mouth. Telling your baby to stop drooling doesn't help. He needs to learn what it feels like to swallow and how it feels to have the mouth area dry. A physical or occupational therapist or a speech therapist can help you learn how to help the baby feel the muscles of the tongue and mouth better and learn to swallow. If your baby is older than 8 months and still drooling a lot get someone to help you teach the baby to feel what it feels like to swallow.

Desensitization

Especially when there are so many other things to talk to the doctor about it is easy for you and the doctor to forget to protect your baby with immunizations.

IMMUNIZATIONS THAT YOUR BABY NEEDS

Diphtheria
Tetanus
Whooping Cough   (usually called DPT)

    1ST   _____(2 months)
    2ND   _____(4 months)
    3RD   _____(6 months)
    4TH   _____(18 months)
Diphtheria
Tetanus
    BOOSTER   _____(4-6 years)
    ADULT BOOSTER   _____(14-16 years)
    ADULT BOOSTER   _____(every 10 years)

Polio
    1ST   _____(2 months)
    2ND   _____(4 months)
    3RD   _____(12 to 16 months)
    BOOSTER   _____(4-6 years)
Mumps
                                       _____(after 12 months) ⎤
German Measles   ⎥ usually given
                                       _____(after 12 months) ⎬ together
                                                                        ⎥
Measles   ⎥
                                       _____(15 months)   ⎦
Flu Immunizations
                                       _____(doctor recom-
                                                        mendation)
Tuberculin Test
at about one year   _____and thereafter
                                                        when exposed

II

You May Be Concerned About Feeding Problems

FEEDING TIME IS USUALLY A FUN TIME FOR BABY AND MOTHER

But if your baby is having trouble eating it may not be fun for either of you.

Since much of the time that you spend with your baby will be feeding time, it is important for both you and the baby that it be as pleasant a time as possible.

Have a comfortable place to sit. In the early months an overstuffed chair or a rocking chair would be nice.

Gather all the things that you need, bottle, spoon, washcloth, and food.

Then try to sit and relax with your baby.

Have some of your favorite music playing.
Slip off your shoes and you may want to take the phone off the hook or make sure that your feeding place is close enough to the phone that you don't have to get up to answer.

1 SOME BABIES HAVE TROUBLE MAKING THEIR MOUTHS SUCK AND SWALLOW

In order to be able to suck and swallow the child must be able to close the lips tightly and push the tongue up and back. Some babies' mouths are not strong enough to move the muscles that way. A therapist or a nurse would call this oral motor problems and could show you how to touch and rub the baby's mouth so the baby's muscles could feel how to work.

Some babies won't nurse or they bite when they start to nurse. For some babies closing the mouth is very difficult and when they close their mouths they close so tightly that they bite the nipple. This is a problem for bottle babies, but more of a problem for a mother who is nursing the baby. What the baby needs to learn is how to close the mouth gently. It helps for the baby to get used to closing the mouth gently but firmly by rubbing the lips and inside the mouth in short even strokes from the cheeks. chin, and nose to the lips. A therapist can show you how to do this.

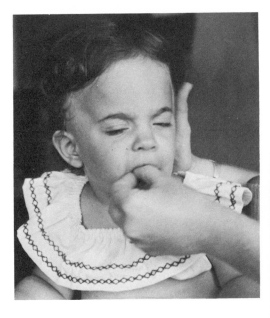

Oral Desensitization

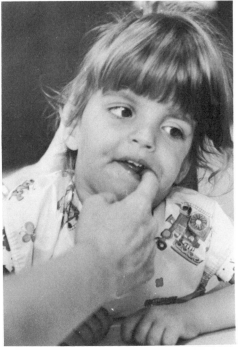

BREAST FEEDING BABIES WHO HAVE TROUBLE SUCKING MAY TAKE SOME EXTRA EFFORT

Your child may tire from sucking and you may need to stop and rub his mouth and cheeks several times during the feeding. You may need to have shorter, more frequent feeding times. You may also need some special cream to put on the nipples so they won't become sore. The article, by Lois Ellis, "Nursing a Baby with Down's Syndrome" in *The Exceptional Parent*, June 1977, may be interesting to you.

SOME BABIES GO TO SLEEP WHILE THEY ARE EATING

Sometimes special babies have to work so hard at sucking that they suck for a little while and then go to sleep. If you put him to bed it is likely that he will wake in a few minutes and want to eat again.

Some infants who didn't weigh much when they were born or who are having trouble gaining weight need to eat more frequently so you should plan small and frequent feedings.

It also helps to be sure that you feed the baby well each time.

Be sure that you burp the baby frequently. Some babies need to be burped several times during the feeding session.

You can burp the traditional way by putting a clean diaper on your shoulder and then holding the baby so he looks over your shoulder and then gently patting his back.

You can also burp the baby by holding him in a sitting position and supporting his head with your hand under the chin and patting the back.

One of these ways will probably work best for you. The baby will probably do better if you use the same way each time.

If someone else feeds him it is a good idea to have them burp the baby the same way you do.

If the baby starts to fuss and cries before you begin to feed him it is likely that he has swallowed some air and the air in the stomach may make him feel full. You may need to burp him before you start to feed him.

Some babies get the food in their mouths, but don't swallow and when they open their mouths, the food comes out again. The baby is probably not really closing the mouth and pushing the food to the back of the mouth, ready to swallow.

For most people the tongue pushes the food to the back of the mouth so it can be swallowed.

For some babies the tongue, instead of pushing the food back, pushes the food forward and it comes out again.

THIS PROBLEM IS CALLED TONGUE THRUST AND IT MEANS THAT FEEDING THE BABY WILL BE A LONG, LONG SLOW PROCESS

A THERAPIST CAN SHOW YOU HOW TO PUT THE FOOD CAREFULLY AT THE SIDE OF THE MOUTH AND HOW TO HELP THE MUSCLES OF THE MOUTH MOVE CORRECTLY BY RUBBING AND APPLYING PRESSURE IN CERTAIN PLACES

The improvement is gradual because learning how to use the tongue is difficult.

You may need some music to entertain you.
You might have some light reading propped up on a book stand to read between bites.

Although it is important to talk to the child with tongue thrust while he is eating, talking to him while he is trying to swallow could make it more difficult for him to use the oral muscles.

Talk to the baby while you are filling the spoon and then let him concentrate while the food is in the mouth.

Be sure that the baby is sitting correctly (see page 29). It is not possible for him to swallow if the head and neck are not in the proper relationship to each other.

A POSITION FOR FEEDING

Some babies choke easily. If he is not able to swallow smoothly, it is easier for the baby to choke.

He is more likely to choke when you are feeding him lying down or sitting without the neck and jaw in an upright position.

The best treatment for choking or gagging too easily is to make the mouth less sensitive by touching firmly on the inside of the mouth and on the tongue. A therapist can show you how to do this.

(See Desensitization, page 25)

*Some babies have learned that choking
makes people pay attention and they
choke on foods that they don't like.*

When babies first begin to drink from a cup
the drink slides down the sides of the
mouth.

There is a plastic cup with a lid and a spout
that can be helpful in learning to close
the mouth and swallow. For special babies it is harder to learn.

This is true because the baby frequently has
not really learned to close the lips and
hold them shut. It may be helpful to have
him drink from a straw bottle that you
can put together for him.

Get a plastic bottle with a lid that has a spout.
Get a piece of plastic tube like that used
in aquarium filters. Cut the top of the
bottle carefully and insert the tube, so it
fits tightly. Cut both ends of the tube at a
diagonal and have the one inside rest at
the bottom of the bottle. Let the other
end extend out about 6 inches. Because
the bottle is airtight you can squeeze the
fluid up close to the baby's mouth and
the baby can suck the fluid into the
mouth. This way the baby can continue
to learn to close the mouth, suck, and
swallow even in a sitting position.

2 SOME BABIES HAVE TROUBLE SITTING UP TO EAT

If the baby's head falls back or forward or to one side when he tries to sit up to eat, he needs to have some special support.

The baby should be sitting with the legs and trunk at right angles and the head and neck in a straight line with the chin tucked toward the chest.

A special chair can be built for the baby by getting instructions from a therapist or props and support can be made for an ordinary chair.

It is possible to purchase a plastic insert that fits on the bottom of the high chair and has a plastic block that fits between the baby's legs to keep him from sliding out.

Often a baby needs a seat belt. You can tie a diaper around him, making sure that it is low by the hip joints rather than up against the stomach or ribs. Or you can make one from heavy duty Velcro that can be purchased from a medical supply house.

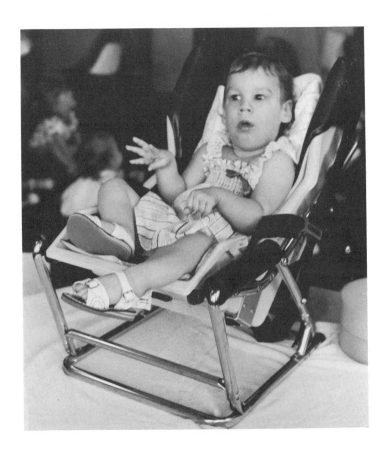

If your baby has cerebral palsy, you could contact the United Cerebral Palsy or Easter Seal Society. In some localities they loan equipment for the family to use with the child.

Sometimes the baby closes the mouth so tight that the spoon cannot be taken out of the mouth. The baby's sensitive mouth is stimulated so much by the spoon and the food that the response is too strong. It helps to use a spoon that is coated. You can get one at a variety store.

It also helps to feed the baby in a quiet place.

It also helps to let the baby know when food is going to be placed in the mouth.

If the food is placed in the side of the mouth it is less likely that the child will bite the spoon.

ALTERNATE FEEDING METHODS

Some babies have so much trouble learning to suck and swallow that they are fed in different ways. Some babies are fed by a tube that goes through the throat area to the stomach. Other babies are fed with a syringe that pushes the food into the digestive system. And some are fed a liquid by a needle in the vein. It may be necessary to feed your baby one of these ways when he is sick.

But it is not wise to continue feeding an alternate way beyond a brief emergency. The baby's mouth and digestive system develop by being used for eating. If you do not teach your baby to eat regular food, the mouth, teeth, and digestive system will not develop properly.

FEEDING THE BABY AT THE TABLE WITH THE REST OF THE FAMILY IS IMPORTANT
THE BABY NEEDS TO LEARN TO BE AROUND OTHERS
THE FAMILY NEEDS TO FEEL THAT THE BABY BELONGS

But it may be that you need to spend so much time feeding the baby that it is difficult to feed the rest of the family.

Other members of the family could help you with the serving. Or you could feed the baby just before the rest of the family and let him sit at the table with finger foods while the rest of the family eat (see page 33).

3 SOME BABIES HAVE TROUBLE HOLDING A SPOON

All babies have trouble learning how to make the spoonful of food get to the mouth. Some babies have more trouble.

If your baby can suck and swallow when you hold the spoon but is not able to get the spoon to the mouth you might need to feed him for most of the meal then let him practice when he is not so hungry.

It is also easier to get food to the mouth with the fingers than with a spoon. At each feeding time and sometimes in between give your baby some dry cereal that is not presweetened and let him practice the hand to mouth movement.

SOME BABIES WANT TO EAT EVERYTHING, EVEN LIQUIDS, WITH THEIR HANDS

Eating with the hands is called "finger feeding." Most babies begin to feed themselves by just picking things up and putting them in their mouths. This is a perfectly natural beginning.

It can become a problem for a special baby when the baby does not seem to be interested in trying to use a spoon.

It is more important for the child to learn the hand to mouth patterns than it is for the eating to be presentable.

Even though your special baby may be messy and have food on the chair, table, and floor it is most important for the baby to learn to finger feed.

The baby must learn to finger feed before he is ready to learn to eat neatly.

SELF FEEDING IS A MESS

You can protect yourself and your baby from the mess by

> Wearing coverup aprons or washable clothes at feeding time (even father when he is helping),
> Having the baby protected with a good bib (one with arms in it would be good),
> Having the floor protected with a plastic cover (purchased by the yard or a plastic table-cloth),
> Allowing the baby to handle the food only while he is attempting to eat the food.

If the baby begins to just play in the food or throw the food take the food away and say: "Food is for eating" without scolding or other comments. Wash the baby and clean up the eating area.
Don't scold the baby or worry about him being hungry. If he were still hungry he would still be eating.

IF THE WHOLE FAMILY IS GOING TO GRANDMOTHER'S OR A GOOD FRIEND'S HOUSE, TAKE THE CHAIR, BIB, PLASTIC, REGULAR SPOON, AND DISH

Or if you do not know the hostess you may choose to let the baby do the real eating at home and just have a "snack" at the house using foods that are "acceptable" finger foods, such as

french fries	apple slices
carrot sticks	crackers or toast

You will have to use your judgment. Of course you do not want to be embarrassed, but you do not want to be isolated just because the special baby needs some time to learn to look "presentable" during meals.

If you decide to go, try to relax and enjoy yourself. You deserve to have a good time, just like everybody else. Try to do the best you can to keep the baby from bothering others, but if your family or friends are uncomfortable about your baby's eating habits let that be their problem.

SOME CHILDREN PLAY WITH THEIR FOOD AND SPILL IT ALL OVER THEMSELVES AND THE EATING AREA

When your child spills food while he is learning to get it to his mouth, he is not doing it purposely.

You will have to put up with some spilled food during the learning time.

but you can change the child's behavior if he has learned to drop or throw food **to get attention.**

Watch closely when he throws or drops food.
Is it food the child doesn't like?
Is he not very hungry?
Is he tired?
Does he enjoy seeing you get mad?

When the child begins to throw or drop food, take it away.
*He may cry—**but don't give in.***
It took a while for him to learn the throwing/dropping routine that gets such an interesting response from you.
It will take a while for him to learn that you are not going to get upset anymore.

Try to feed your child before you are both too tired—
and try to be calm—
even when you take food away and he fusses or when daddy or grandmother wants you to give in.

Remember—*If your child was still hungry, he would still be eating.*

4 SOME BABIES HAVE TROUBLE EATING WHEN OTHERS FEED THEM

IN MOST FAMILIES THE BABY WILL BE THE MOST COMFORTABLE WHEN MOTHER DOES THE FEEDING

Even though the mother may later go to work and have someone else care for the baby most of the day, she is the one who usually feeds the baby from the beginning and they develop a "working relationship."

ALTHOUGH THE PATTERN OF THE MOTHER AND BABY "WORKING TOGETHER" ON THE FEEDING IS A GOOD ONE,

it is also important that the baby learn to eat when someone else is doing the feeding.

LEARNING TO EAT WITH OTHERS IS AN IMPORTANT PART OF LEARNING TO GET ALONG WITH OTHERS

If it is possible for the father to be around at the hectic evening mealtime it would be an excellent time for father and baby to learn to "work together" on feeding.

Babies tend to respond better to those who feed and bathe them than to the people they see at less important times.

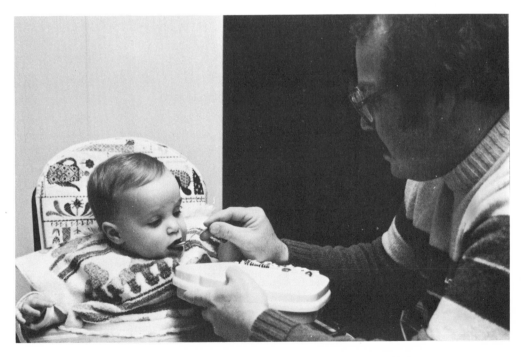

LEARNING TO FEED THE BABY IS FATHER'S OPPORTUNITY TO LEARN TO KNOW THE BABY.

In order for the baby not to be confused the father (or other person) who assists the mother with the feeding should hold the baby or sit him the same way the mother does and use the same bibs, spoons, and chairs—and try to feed the same way.

For the baby to be comfortable both the mother and father must be pleasant and comfortable about the feeding arrangement.

This is the family's chance to have the father become part of the baby's daily life and for the mother to learn to "let go" a little.

5 SOME PEOPLE HAVE TROUBLE EATING CERTAIN FOODS

Some problems that special children have make it necessary to avoid certain foods.
Some have trouble assimilating proteins and cannot have milk or milk products. (Make sure that the doctor has checked your baby for PKU.) If babies cannot drink cows' milk, they need to have a special formula.

IF YOUR CHILD HAS A RESTRICTED DIET, IT IS VERY IMPORTANT THAT YOU FOLLOW IT EXACTLY.

Although you may feel that your child is "missing" some nice things and you may want to give him some foods that he should not have, don't give in, even for a holiday treat!

It will confuse your child to have foods one time and not to be able to have them another. If he has never had the foods, he won't miss them. In fact, he may not even like a taste that is unusual to him.

CHILDREN MAY GET HIVES OR A RASH FROM EATING SUCH THINGS AS:

tomatoes, oranges, spices, artificially flavored foods, and presweetened foods.

If your baby has had rashes and hives, it is important to feed him only one new food at a time Keep a record of when you started to feed each new food. The reaction to the food may not appear for several days. Don't start another new food for at least two weeks, then you can tell which food bothers your child.

You may think this kind of eating will be boring to your child but remember that all foods are new to him although you may have been eating those foods for years.

There are some books about babies' and children's diet that may be helpful to you:

Smith, L. *Feed Your Kids Right*, Delta Books, New York, 1979.
Smith, L. *Improving Your Child's Behavior Chemistry*, Pocket Books, New York, 1976.
Larson, G. *Better Food for Better Babies*, Keats Pub., New Canaan, Connecticut, 1972.

Baby's Food Record

New Food	Date Fed	Amount Eaten	Immediate Reaction	Later Reaction

Even when they later learn to like the food

MOST BABIES DON'T LIKE NEW FOODS

They usually pull back and make a face when
they are given unfamiliar foods.

Babies who have problems learning may
have more problems learning to like
new foods.

**But you still don't want the baby to miss
foods that are nutritionally important.**

BE SURE THAT WHAT THE BABY IS HAVING TROUBLE LEARNING TO LIKE IS REALLY
IMPORTANT TO HIS HEALTH

Try giving him small portions when you know
that he is both hungry and happy and

So food won't   to be thawed quickly and
used one   the refrigerator again and
again.

IF YOUR BAE   ) IT MAY BE A SIGN THAT
FEEDIN

It's probabl   *t only makes a mess, but*
makes

Try to be ca

It may also b   e what goes into his mouth.

It may be a

If your baby has motor problems (see page 53) it may be too difficult for him to move the hand to the mouth. You could still let him choose what to eat by showing him what you were going to feed and asking "Do you want some cereal?" then and watching closely his response.

BABIES WILL EAT STRANGE THINGS: DIRT, DUST, CLAY, ROCKS, SAND, PAPER, TOOTHPASTE, SOAP, DOGFOOD, AND EVEN FECES

Of course you don't want your baby to do this, but don't be alarmed if he does.

The baby's taste buds are not as well trained as the adults and they do not taste the difference in foods and other things. Babies respond to food and other things in their mouths from the texture and temperature rather than from the flavor. The coldness of ice cream is less appealing to the baby who is used to warm milk than it is to the adult who is used to having cold milk and iced drinks.

When they are just learning, babies explore by putting things in their mouths. They chew rattles and teethers and anything else.

Just because the baby puts the object into his mouth does not mean that he understands or plans to eat it.

Perhaps the best way to keep him from putting strange things into his mouth is to keep those things out of reach.

When he does put something in the mouth that you don't want there, calmly remove the object. You may need to use your finger if the material has broken into small pieces. Say coolly, "No, No," and give him something that can go into the mouth.

SOME BABIES SEEM TO BE ABLE TO EAT AND EAT AND WILL STILL ACCEPT MORE FOOD IF IT IS GIVEN TO THEM

They enjoy the feeling of food in the mouth and stomach but do not seem to feel the sensation of being "full."

If your child has these problems, feed him as much as you think he needs, then clean him up and put the food away.

If he is feeding himself, give the child an adequate amount and put the remaining food away.

If the baby does not want to give up eating, offer a favorite toy or some interesting quiet activity just after eating.

Smile, but be firm.

DON'T GIVE IN BY ALLOWING "JUST A LITTLE MORE"

Overweight babies have more difficulty learning to move and explore.

If your baby has difficulty learning what it feels like to be full, help him learn to eat a reasonable amount then to stop eating.

ELIMINATION PROBLEMS MAY BEGIN WITH FEEDING PROBLEMS

Bowel movement means movement of a set of muscles. If your baby has trouble moving arms and legs, it is likely that he will have trouble moving bowels, too.

Learning to move the muscles of the trunk is necessary for regular elimination (see pages 5 and 6).

For some babies the bowels need to move several times a day.

Others may be healthy with a bowel movement every two or three days.

It will be easier to develop a regular pattern if the baby's diet includes fruits and cereals.

If your child has loose stools, check the food record and see if he has eaten new foods.

Medication can also cause elimination problems.

Don't try to make all of these decisions yourself. Ask your doctor about the baby's feeding and elimination problems.

ALL BABIES SPIT UP SOMETIMES

And your baby will spit up sometimes after eating.

BUT IF YOUR BABY ALWAYS SPITS UP,

or gags or swallows several times to get the food down or vomits after eating; the baby's esophagus may be partly or completely blocked so the food can't get to his stomach.

If your family doctor is not sure about the cause, ask to be referred to a specialist. The baby may have esophageal regurgitation.

The doctor may want to suture the esophagus so the parts stay in place during digestion.

Many therapists also suggest that the position of feeding can help the baby keep from vomiting.

Generally speaking, if a child is fed only liquids or semi-liquids in a horizontal position, he will be more likely to have difficulty keeping the food down. A therapist with special training in feeding techniques can show you how to hold and feed your baby.

INFANTS AND CHILDREN CAN ALSO DEVELOP ULCERS

6 DEHYDRATION

It is important that your baby have sufficient intake of fluids especially when he has diarrhea, has been vomiting, or it is extremely hot.

Give juices and water frequently.

When loss of water from the body is more than the intake of fluids, the body does not have enough fluid to create mucus, urine, lymph, and other body fluids.

If your baby takes medication it is especially important that there be plenty of fluids in the baby's system.

If your child has diarrhea and is vomiting, he may need more than just liquids.

See your doctor about other substances that the baby may need—or see your doctor if he keeps throwing up the liquids. 7-Up or other carbonated drinks will often stay down when other things will not. Milk is very hard for a baby to keep down when he has been throwing up.

If your baby does not have proper fluid replacement he will become dehydrated.

7 YOUR CHILD MAY NEED MEDICATION

When your doctor prescribes medication for your child make sure you give the medication as directed. It is important that the child have the amount that it prescribed at the time that it is prescribed.

NEVER GIVE MORE MEDICATION THAN THE DOCTOR PRESCRIBES

If the problem doesn't seem to be getting better as quickly as you think that it should

CALL THE DOCTOR

The doctor will tell you if more medication will help.

Be sure that you measure the amounts carefully and report to the doctor if the child becomes fussy or gets a rash after taking the medication.

Some medications that your doctor may prescribe might cause other side effects for your baby.

Some of these are:
  drowsy or sleepy much of the time
  cranky or irritable
  awake and unable to sleep
  not wanting to eat
  not wanting to drink
  wanting to eat all the time
  nausea
  diarrhea or constipation

Some medications may have more long term side effects such as:
  soreness around the teeth and growth
    of the gums around or over the teeth
  swelling in the face and neck

Your doctor will need to know what these are and when they started and how severe they are in order to decide what needs to be done about them.

If your baby is taking medication for long term problems, such as epilepsy or hydrocephalus your doctor will probably want to test the blood to see how much of the medication is retained in the child's body. This will help determine the exact dose that will be most beneficial

Sometimes the side effect is caused because the baby is already getting some medication when the doctor prescribes the new medication and the mixture of the two in the baby's body causes problems.

ALWAYS TELL THE DOCTOR ABOUT ANY MEDICATION THAT YOUR CHILD IS TAKING

Even if another doctor prescribed it or if you think that the over-the-counter cough medicine is not very strong. When the two medications are mixed together it can cause the baby's body some real problems.

III

You May Be Concerned About Sleep Problems

Since most babies sleep a lot, it is natural to assume that sleeping is something that a baby knows when born.

THAT ISN'T TRUE—THE BABY MUST LEARN HOW, WHEN, AND WHERE TO SLEEP

Time spent asleep alternates with time spent awake.

For the young infant the times are almost equal.

Sleep–wake, sleep–wake—each part lasts a few hours.

For adults the pieces of the cycle are longer.

The adult is awake for a longer time and asleep for a longer time.

As the baby grows, the cycles of sleep and waking become more like the adult. Some of the problems that parents have with babies' sleep are because the sleep and wake patterns are short.

BUT BABIES CAN ALSO HAVE SLEEP PROBLEMS

Some babies are extra sensitive to sounds and temperature and wake easily if they change.

Some babies cannot sleep unless they have their own bed.

Some babies are sensitive to the moods of others around them and cannot sleep if the parents are anxious.

Babies will go to sleep easier and stay asleep longer if the parents are relaxed and expect the baby to sleep.

Some children have trouble learning to sleep for long periods and then be awake for long periods, they just take cat naps even at night.

Some babies will sleep only if they are rocked—that may be not just because the baby is relaxed, but because you are relaxed, too.

Some babies will only go to sleep when they rock themselves back and forth or bounce the head again and again against the pillow.

That might be the only way they know how to relax (see Health Problems, 2).

1 IF THE BABY DOESN'T SLEEP WELL, PARENTS SOMETIMES TAKE HIM TO THEIR BED

As the baby gets older sometimes the parents get a bed for the baby in their room in case the child has problems in the night.

THIS IS NOT A GOOD PRACTICE FOR THE BABY OR FOR THE PARENT

Parents who have a child in the bedroom all the time are not able to talk to each other or enjoy intimate relationships.

In order for parents to have a comfortable home to raise the baby they need time to be alone together and they need a place that is private.

If the baby has continuing health problems such as seizures (see Health Problems, 1) or breathing problems (see Health Problems, 4), you may want to have a one-way window installed then arrange the baby's room so you could see the bed easily and check on the baby without leaving your room.

If the baby's room is adjacent to yours and the window is carefully placed, you could see while you were standing up or still in your bed.

Some families monitor the baby's room with a TV or intercom system. Inexpensive, portable sets are available at Radio Shack.

If you live in an apartment, place the baby's room as close to your room as possible but avoid having the baby sleep in your room or your bed.

Having the child sleep in your room not only affects your relationship with each other but it will be telling the baby that you do not expect him to sleep well and that you expect him to stay dependent.

2 SOME BABIES HAVE TROUBLE LEARNING WHEN TO SLEEP

When you are feeding the baby and he stops sucking and goes to sleep then wakes again when you have put him to bed, he may have fallen asleep because effort that it took to nurse was enough to exhaust him.

Continue working with the therapist to find ways to help strengthen the baby's mouth muscles (see Feeding Problems, 1).

FEED THE BABY BEFORE HE GETS TOO TIRED

and keep gently waking him up to encourage better feeding.

When he is able to eat more, he will be able to sleep longer.

If the baby sleeps all day and is awake all night, try to encourage a change in the pattern by not putting him to bed during the day and keeping him near where you are working.

Then make the baby comfortable at night and leave him in a dark room in bed when he wakes, rather than picking him up at the slightest whimper.

MANY SPECIAL CHILDREN ARE RESTLESS SLEEPERS AND WAKE EASILY

Sometimes during an illness a child needs a cool bath to reduce fever (see Health Problems, 5) or an enema or other special care that might make him uncomfortable.

At those times, you may need to hold your child or rock him to sleep.

It is important to do this only when your child doesn't feel well and then only as long as he is really sick.

He can get used to it in a day or two.

A child who is more independent will not need rocking all the time—but one with special problems can easily learn to become dependent.

If your child is so restless at night that you are concerned, it may be wise for one of the parents to sleep in the child's room on a cot or on the floor rather than putting the child in the parent's room.

Even special babies, however, do not need to have a parent sleeping in the room with them all the time.

3 SOMETIMES THE BABY DOESN'T FEEL LIKE SLEEPING

Some special babies will lie in bed and look at the ceiling without crying for hours. It is important to watch during the day and when the child is awake, bring him where more things are happening.

If the baby just lies in bed he will not be learning about other people or how to interact with them.

PUT THE BABY TO BED ONLY WHEN IT IS A TIME THAT THE BABY USUALLY SLEEPS OR IT IS A TIME THAT THE BABY SHOULD BE SLEEPING
DO NOT USE THE CRIB FOR A "PLAY PEN" OR A SAFE PLACE TO PUT THE BABY WHILE YOU DO OTHER THINGS

You may need a safe play area, or a play pen, but have it out in the part of the house where the baby can observe family activities.

FREQUENTLY SPECIAL BABIES WILL NOT GO TO SLEEP UNLESS THEY ARE IN THEIR OWN BED

All babies have this problem sometimes, but babies who are facing one new thing after another, frequently cannot be comfortable enough to go to sleep in any place but their own bed with their own blankets.

If you need to take the child somewhere to sleep, you may be able to take the bed, or at least the bedding.

It would be wise to arrange your affairs so the baby doesn't need to be away from his familiar room and bed during a crisis, but it is also important that he learn to sleep away from home.

Before there is an emergency help him learn to sleep away from home. Try overnight in a friendly home. Grandparents are usually patient enough. The baby is likely to fuss that night. Don't give up. Keep at it regularly.

If you do not teach your baby to be comfortable sleeping away from home, you and your family will be unnecessarily restricted on vacation and travel plans. Staying home just for the baby is a foolish burden.

USUALLY BABIES SLEEP WELL IN THE CAR
  SOMETIMES PARENTS TAKE THE BABY FOR A RIDE JUST TO GET HIM TO SLEEP

This can be a time-consuming practice and a real chore.

Taking him for a walk or doing finger plays with him may be a more effective way of getting the baby tired enough to sleep.

It is important that the pre-sleep plan not be too rough and exciting since it is possible to stimulate a child so much that he will not be able to relax enough to sleep.

Although there will be interruptions when unexpected visitors come or when there is a family emergency and the routines must be altered, it is wise to create a bedtime and to stick to it.

The special baby needs to go to bed at the same time and in the same place as much as possible.

The baby will learn when and where to sleep if you put him to bed in the same bed at the same time with the same "teddy bear" night after night.

Having the same playtime just before bedtime is also nice. It is a particularly good time for a play time with daddy.

4 SOMETIMES PARENTS WORRY BECAUSE THE CHILD SLEEPS TOO MUCH OR TOO LONG

When your child does not wake up at the usual time, it is natural to be concerned and to go check on him.

If your child has been sleeping at regular times and nothing has interrupted the routine, then it would be wise to gently wake him up and feed, bathe, or play with him as usual.

If the child's routine is interrupted, he may need extra sleep.

The routine could be interrupted by:

a. Being sick, (sick babies need more rest)
b. The mother or usual caregiver being away, (this is stressful, thus the child requires more sleep)
c. The family going on a trip (after a trip everyone needs more rest, especially children)
d. Having house guests (the stimulation is tiring)
e. Unusually cold or hot weather (causes physical stress)

All of these situations occur naturally and you will not want to protect your child from everyday life. (Even childhood diseases help the baby build immunity to ever-present germs.) You should be sure, however, that he gets the amount of rest that he needs.

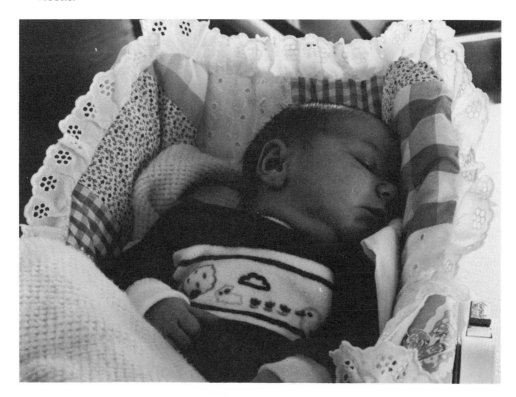

SOME CHILDREN GO TO SLEEP WHEN THEY ARE BORED OR WHEN THEY ARE NOT ABLE TO UNDERSTAND THE SITUATION

Sleep is the condition in which the body relaxes because it is no longer trying to pay attention.

Sometimes babies who have trouble seeing, hearing, understanding, and knowing what they should be doing, go to sleep to avoid the confusion caused by things they don't understand.

If your child seems to be going to sleep at parties, during outings, when you are talking to friends, or at other times that are pleasant for you, try to look at the experience from his point of view.

It may be that at those times you are not giving him the usual amount of attention and he doesn't understand why things are different or how to ask for attention.

Of course it would not be wise for you to give up all the things you enjoy, but you may be able to help your child feel more comfortable if you watch him from the corner of your eye, talk to him, and show him things while you are talking to friends or shopping.

Other times you might get a babysitter and enjoy these experiences for yourself.

SOME BABIES NEED TO BE MOVED IN THEIR SLEEP

Since parents of special babies need to be more careful, it is easy to become concerned about the baby while he is sleeping and want to check to see if he is all right.

If you feel that you need to check then it is wise to do so, but if you turn on the lights and go in loudly and touch or turn the baby over you may disrupt the sleeping pattern.

If your baby has cerebral palsy or has difficulty making the normal movements and adjustments during sleep, it is wise for you to go quietly to the baby and move him from one side to the other or from tummy to side several times during the night or the nap. A therapist can show you some good sleeping positions and tell you how often to move the baby.

If you go in to move the baby do so with lights dim and without noise or talking to the baby so there will be as little disturbance as possible.

Water beds for children with severe cerebral palsy can be very useful. The temperature control is maintained. There will be no pressure points which break down skin, and rocking from minor movements made by the child are pleasant sensations.

CHANGING SLEEP ROUTINES

As the child develops, less sleep will be needed,
> **but the change will be gradual,**
> and it will effect the routine very little.
> **there will never be a need for an abrupt change.**

If you want to change something in the sleep pattern, do it slowly and gradually.

If you want to rearrange the room, start by moving the dresser or chair, then piece-by-piece move the other furniture. Don't change the bedding at the same time.

If a favorite teddy bear and blanket both look worn, try adding a new teddy bear for a few days or weeks, then have the old one "disappear." Do the same with the blanket. Do them one-at-a-time—slowly. Change is difficult, even for adults, and more difficult for children. For special children it is even more difficult.

IV

You May Be Concerned About Motor/Movement Problems

1 SOME BABIES ARE LISTLESS AND DO NOT MOVE MUCH

A THERAPIST WOULD CALL THIS HAVING "LOW TONE"

It means that the muscles do not know how to pull firm and hold that position.

IF SOMEONE ELSE MOVES THE BABY, THE ARMS AND LEGS ARE FLOPPY AND THE HEAD BOBS FORWARD, BACKWARD, AND TO THE SIDE

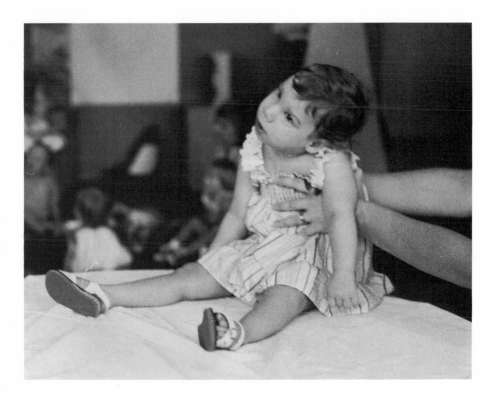

A baby whose arms and legs and head flop around is hard to bathe, dress, and feed.

If you try to make him sit he will usually lean to one side, roll to that side, and fall over.

If you try to hold him up to stand, the legs bend and fold when you try to put his weight on them.

In order for the baby to learn to control the body he will need to learn to feel the parts of the body as they move.

He will need activities that make him feel as "awake" as possible.

YOU CAN HELP YOUR BABY BE ALERT BY CARRYING HIM AROUND WITH YOU SO HE CAN LEARN TO ADJUST TO MOVEMENT.

Hold the baby in the air and turn him over.

Tickle and touch him.

Talk to him.

Let the baby play in water.

Be sure he has things to touch that have texture and color.

Sing to him.

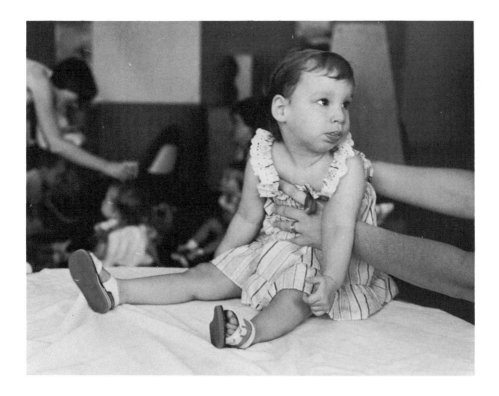

Take the baby for a walk in the stroller.

Swing him in the porch swing.

Attract his attention with bright, noisy toys.

SOMETIMES THIS IS CALLED INFANT STIMULATION

A physical or occupational therapist who has worked with babies can help you.

A nurse or a teacher who has worked with babies can help you.

They can show you some of the ways to move your baby and some of the things to do with him that might be particularly good to help him learn how to make more firmness in the muscles.

These books may also help you:

Finnie, N. R. *Handling the Young Cerebral Palsied Child at Home*, 2nd Edition, E. P. Dutton, New York, 1974 and 1975. This book gives detailed information about how to move and take care of a child with cerebral palsy. It shows diagrams of ways to hold and play with the child as well as simple equipment to make.

Hansen, M. J. *Teaching Your Down's Syndrome Infant*, University Park Press, Baltimore, 1978. This book describes ways to help the Down's syndrome infant understand things that are happening.

Levy, J. *Baby Exercise Book: The First Fifteen Months*, Pantheon, New York, 1974. This book shows some of the ways that you can move your baby while you are taking care of him that will help him develop.

Painter, G. *Teach Your Baby*, Simon & Schuster, New York, 1971. This book shows pictures of how to play with your baby and how to help your baby understand what is happening.

2 SOME BABIES ARE STIFF AND IT IS HARD TO BEND THE JOINTS

A THERAPIST WOULD CALL THIS HAVING "HIGH TONE"

That means that the muscles do not know how to relax and allow the body to bend and move.

JOINTS MOVE BECAUSE THE MUSCLES AROUND THEM ARE FLEXIBLE

Some babies have trouble moving because their muscles are pulled tight all the time.

A baby whose muscles do not relax easily will frequently straighten arms and legs and push the head back and make the whole body stiff and partly leaning back.

When the muscles are tight the baby will be stiff and not able to move the joints. It is not possible for him to turn over, or bend or move.

You can learn some ways to help break up this body pattern of stiff muscles so you can move the baby to bathe, dress, and feed him.

You will need a therapist to tell you exactly what to do with your baby, but the books listed on page 56 have some parts that will be helpful for you.

JOINTS AND MUSCLES IN BABIES ARE STILL DEVELOPING
    IF THEY DO NOT MOVE WHILE THEY ARE DEVELOPING
    THEY GROW TO BE STIFF OR THEY GROW TO BE TWISTED

To prevent the joints from growing stiff or crooked the body has to move.

If the baby can't move his body himself, he needs someone to help him move so his body will grow and develop normally.

A physical or occupational therapist can show you how the body is designed to move and how to hold your baby so the joints will be flexed and can continue to develop normally and be moveable.

THIS WILL NOT MEAN JUST MOVING THE ARMS AND LEGS THROUGH THE NORMAL MOVEMENT
    that they make while the body is resting (called range of motion).

But it also means helping the baby learn normal movement for the trunk of the body.

The movement of the arms and legs is not very useful if the baby can't move his trunk.

Since the body is growing all the time, the treatment for teaching the body to move normally must go on all of the time. Much of the movement you will be able to facilitate while you are bathing, dressing, and feeding the baby. It is important that you do this in the early months and years while the baby's body is growing and developing the most.

IF YOU TRY TO HOLD YOUR BABY THE WAY YOU WOULD HOLD MOST BABIES, HIS BODY WILL GO STIFF AND LEAN BACK

It will probably make you feel that the baby doesn't want to be picked up, when really the baby may be so happy about being picked up that the excitement stimulates his body so much that it goes stiff.

This will happen almost all the time when someone who has not learned how to hold him tries to hold the baby.

WHEN YOU ARE AROUND YOUR BABY TALK TO HIM

IN PLEASANT, NATURAL TONE TELL
YOUR CHILD WHAT YOU PLAN TO DO
BEFORE YOU TOUCH HIM OR PICK
HIM UP

Make sure that your hands are not cold. You
can warm them with warm water or rub
them quickly against your clothes.

TOUCH THE BABY GENTLY—BUT FIRMLY
LIGHT TOUCHING FEELS LIKE
TICKLING
and it will be uncomfortable so he will go
stiff or maybe flop around.

HOLD THE BABY FIRMLY AS YOU LIFT HIM SO HE WILL NOT BE AFRAID OF FALLING
OR SLIDING FROM YOUR ARMS

WHEN YOU HOLD THE BABY, KEEP HIS ARMS AND LEGS
    BENT AND HIS HEAD FORWARD
SUPPORT THE BABY AROUND THE HEAD AND SHOULDERS AND UNDER THE KNEES

IN ORDER TO KEEP THE BABY FROM GOING STIFF IT WILL BE HELPFUL TO TURN HIM
    ON THE SIDE

WHILE HE IS LYING ON HIS SIDE, KEEP HIS BACK STRAIGHT AND HIS HEAD LEANING
    FORWARD
BEND HIS KNEES AND KEEP HIS HANDS IN FRONT OF HIS FACE

Put a small folded blanket or towel under his head and between the baby's knees.

This is called side-lying position.
    It is one of the most important positions for the baby.
    **With part of the body bent or flexed, as the therapists call it, it is less likely that the body
    will push back and be stiff.**

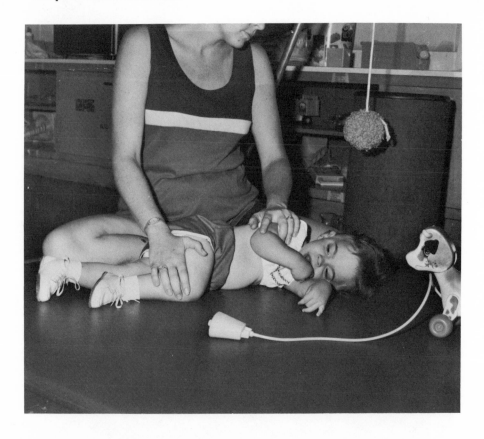

YOU CAN PUT THE BABY IN THE SIDE-LYING POSITION AS YOU ARE STARTING TO
    PICK HIM UP
    and then continue to keep the head forward and knees bent.

IF THE BABY IS QUITE STIFF, YOU MAY NEED TO HOLD FIRMLY TO KEEP HIS LEGS
    FLEXED AND HEAD FORWARD

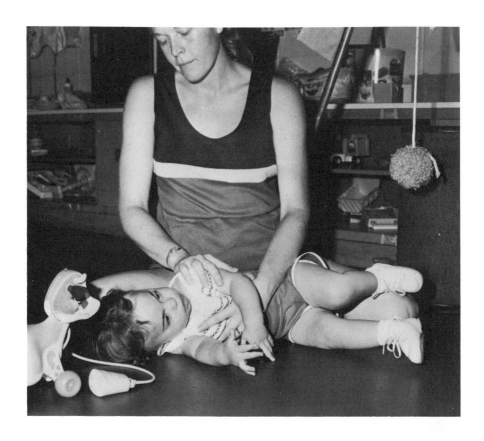

YOU CAN ALSO PUT THE BABY IN SIDE-
    LYING POSITION TO DRESS OR
    FEED

                        SIDE-LYING POSITION IS GOOD FOR
                            SLEEPING

It will be more natural for the baby to lie on the same side all the time.

BUT FOR THE BABY TO DEVELOP EVENLY ON BOTH SIDES, IT IS
    IMPORTANT THAT HE LIE ON BOTH SIDES ABOUT THE SAME AMOUNT OF TIME

So help him use the less favored side—by putting him on that side AT LEAST HALF OF THE
    TIME.

If your baby's body goes stiff when he is picked up,

GRANDPARENTS AND OTHERS MAY BE UNCOMFORTABLE TAKING CARE OF HIM

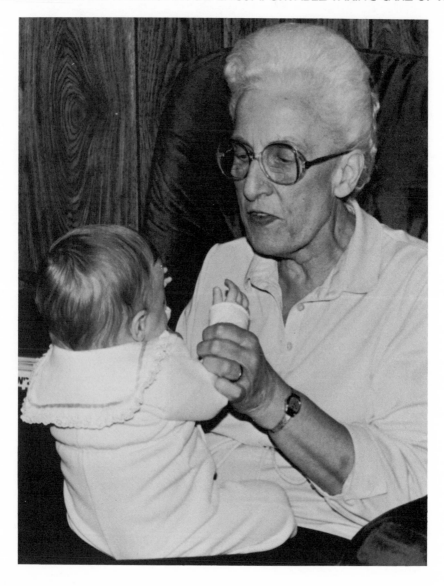

AND YOU MAY BE UNCOMFORTABLE HAVING THEM CARE FOR THE BABY

After you learn to hold the baby

IT IS IMPORTANT TO SHOW GRAND-
   PARENTS

            and others who may be around how to hold
               the baby, so he won't miss the richness

                        OF GETTING TO KNOW AND TRUST
                           OTHER PEOPLE

               When others are to care for your baby

SHOW THEM HOW TO HELP THE BABY
   GET INTO SIDE-LYING POSITION

            LET THE OTHER PERSONS PRACTICE
               WHILE YOU ARE THERE TO HELP
               THEM LEARN

*If you do not help others become comfortable with the baby, then you will be the only one
   who can care for him.*

He will miss learning how to get along with others and others will miss knowing him.

And you will be so tied to him that you will not have

THE OPPORTUNITY FOR REST AND RELAXATION THAT YOU MUST HAVE TO MAIN-
   TAIN YOUR OWN STRENGTH AND EMOTIONAL STABILITY

When your baby is comfortable in side-lying it is time to

HELP HIM LEARN TO MOVE MORE BY HELPING HIM LEARN TO SIDE-SIT

SIDE-SITTING BEGINS BY SIDE-LYING AND THEN
   LIFTING THE SHOULDER UP SO THE BABY IS LEANING

the weight on the elbow. **Be sure that the elbow is directly below the shoulder**. This is called
   side-sitting with support.

IN THIS POSITION THE BABY CAN USE HIS ARMS MORE FREELY

to play with toys or put snack food into his mouth (see Feeding Problems, 3)

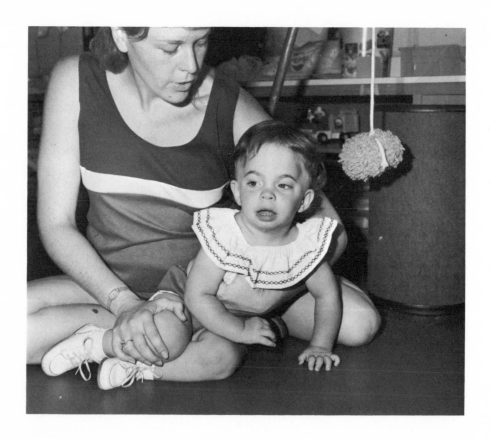

YOUR BABY WILL PROBABLY BE STRONGER ON ONE SIDE

and it will seem that you should let the baby sit on that side most of the time

BUT IF YOU DO, THE STRONG SIDE WILL GET STRONGER AND THE WEAK SIDE WILL GET WEAKER

BE SURE THAT YOU HAVE YOUR BABY SIDE-SIT WITH SUPPORT ON BOTH SIDES

AFTER YOUR BABY IS COMFORTABLE SIDE-SITTING WITH SUPPORT ON BOTH SIDES—GRADUALLY REDUCE THE AMOUNT OF SUPPORT

so the baby is able to learn to sit with his legs to one side and balance by supporting his own weight on the extended arm.

Be sure to have your baby practice this sitting on both sides.

MOST BABIES WHO HAVE TROUBLE LEARNING TO SIT
    WILL BE ABLE TO SIT ON ONE SIDE MUCH EASIER THAN THE OTHER

It will be natural for you to want the baby to sit on the good side all of the time.

If you do this, the baby's body will only develop on the good side.

IF THE BABY HAS TROUBLE SITTING ON ONE SIDE, IT IS MORE IMPORTANT THAN
    EVER TO HAVE THE BABY SIT ON THAT SIDE SO IT WILL DEVELOP AND BECOME
    STRONGER

It won't become stronger, unless he sits on that side so help him to do it.

EVEN IF YOU AND THE BABY DON'T LIKE IT!

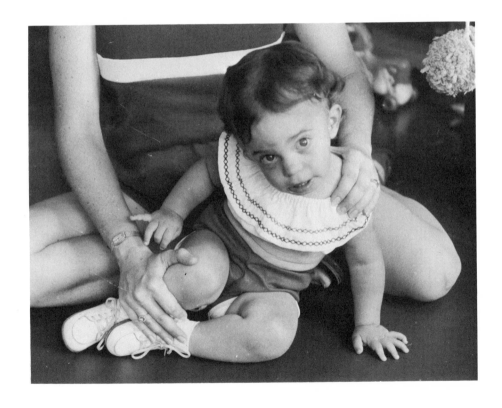

Since the baby can hold his body rigid, it might seem that it would be easier for him to learn to stand up and walk and to skip learning to sit.

BUT IT IS NECESSARY FOR HIM TO LEARN TO BEND AND MOVE
 HIS BODY, TO SIT, TO PULL UP TO STAND
 BEFORE HE CAN LEARN TO MOVE HIS BODY WELL ENOUGH
 TO BALANCE AND WALK

The baby needs to learn to sit before he will
 have enough balance to learn to dress
 and feed by himself.

IF YOU CAN BE PATIENT AND WORK SLOWLY, YOUR BABY WILL LEARN

THERE ARE SOME DAYS WHEN YOUR CHILD WILL BE TIRED OR SICK

If he is tired or sick or upset about something, the baby will be more tense and more stiff and it will be more likely that he will become rigid

THOSE "BAD DAYS" WILL NOT BE GOOD
DAYS TO TEACH SOMEONE ELSE
TO HANDLE THE BABY

unless there is an emergency and it must be
done then.

IF YOU ARE PLANNING A TRIP
OR A NEW BABY IS COMING
OR YOUR SPECIAL BABY
NEEDS SOME SURGERY

start teaching others to handle your baby in
plenty of time, so there won't be a last
minute emergency.

IT MAY TAKE YOUR BABY MUCH LONGER TO LEARN
TO SIT UP AND MOVE WITHOUT HELP

but it is not possible to hurry the process

IT IS NOT POSSIBLE TO LEARN MORE ADVANCED MOVEMENT
UNTIL HE HAS LEARNED
SIDE—LYING
SIDE-SITTING WITH SUPPORT
SIDE-SITTING WITHOUT SUPPORT

A physical therapist or an occupational therapist or a teacher can help you find ways to
practice this movement **in ways that will make it interesting to you and your baby**.

If it seems dull to you—play some of your favorite music or think about going out.

BUT TRY TO MAKE YOUR BABY FEEL THAT YOU ARE PLEASED TO BE WORKING
AND PLAYING WITH HIM

If the baby feels that you like it, he can do a better job.

3 SOME BABIES ARE SOMETIMES LISTLESS AND OTHER TIMES STIFF

Sometimes the body is resting
and the muscles are relaxed

Sometimes the body is moving
and the muscles must be firm

Sometimes the body is working
and the muscles must be tight

THE PERSON ADJUSTS THE MUSCLE TONE TO FIT ACTIVITY

THE CENTRAL NERVOUS SYSTEM OF SOME BABIES IS NOT WELL ENOUGH
ADAPTED TO MAKE THIS ADJUSTMENT ACCURATELY

The baby will sometimes be rigid when the activity requires the muscles to be relaxed.

The baby will sometimes be floppy when the activity requires the muscles to be firm.

The baby will sometimes stay relaxed or firm all the time when the activity requires that muscles are firm for a few seconds then relaxed for a few seconds.

THE BABY WHO HAS MUSCLE TONE THAT CHANGES QUICKLY IS HARD TO HANDLE

Just when you adjust to the baby's tone and think that you are holding him comfortably, the muscle tone changes and the baby slips from your arms—or high chair—or grocery cart.

TO PREVENT THIS, IT MAY BE NECESSARY TO HAVE A SPECIAL SEAT FOR YOUR BABY

A SEAT WITH SUPPORT BETWEEN THE LEGS CAN HELP KEEP THE BABY FROM
SLIPPING

You can purchase a small plastic insert for
the high chair. You can get one from
.... or

YOU CAN MAKE A STRAP THAT GOES
BETWEEN THE BABY'S LEGS

A PHYSICAL OR OCCUPATIONAL THERAPIST CAN SHOW YOU HOW TO
MAKE SOME EQUIPMENT THAT WOULD HELP YOU TAKE CARE OF YOUR BABY

It is natural for you to be uncomfortable and angry when the baby is hard to hold or cannot sit still, but it is important to treat the **change of muscle tone as natural occurence** *and not to scold the baby or become upset.*

It is not something that the baby is doing intentionally.

The book, *Functional Aids for the Multi Handicapped*, edited by Isabel P. Robinault, Harper & Row, New York, 1973, has instructions for helpful equipment.

4   WHEN YOUR BABY HAS TROUBLE DOING THINGS YOU WILL PROBABLY WANT TO DO THE THINGS FOR HIM

If you always do things for your baby,

> HE WILL NOT LEARN TO DO THINGS BY HIMSELF

Naturally you will be uncomfortable when you watch your baby trying to do things and not being able to do them because he can't control his body.

Try not to be embarrassed or scold him.

AND DON'T LET OTHER PEOPLE MAKE FUN OF THE BABY'S AWKWARD MOVEMENTS

When babies are young, certain groups of muscles work together to make the same movement over and over again.

THERAPISTS CALL THESE MOVEMENTS REFLEXES

As the baby gets older he will learn to control his muscles separately and he can make the same movement again, or he can change the movement. The baby learns to **inhibit the reflex movement**. Some babies have trouble learning to do this.

The best way
FOR THE BABY TO LEARN TO CONTROL THE TENSION IN HIS MUSCLES
is to keep
THE SETTING AS RELAXED AS POSSIBLE

THE HARDER THE BABY CONSCIOUSLY TRIES, THE MORE DIFFICULT THE CONTROL WILL BE

Sometimes the baby will be holding so tightly
that he cannot let go of something.

> And sometimes he will drop things.

BE PATIENT AND CALM

If the baby can hold the object sometimes, and he is ready to use the object (see Language and Social Problems) then put it back into his hand.

It will be helpful to have toys, spoons, and bottles made of material that is as light as possible.

Toys that are made for pet birds are often strong, lightweight plastic.

Make sure the toy doesn't have parts that might come loose in the baby's mouth.

IF THE BABY'S MUSCLE TONE CHANGES, THE BABY IS HARD TO HOLD

Since the change in muscle tension will make it hard for you to know how your baby will react to the things that are happening, it will be difficult for you to know when he will be stiff or limp.

You might be talking to the baby or showing him something and his muscle tone may change suddenly, especially when he sees something interesting or hears a loud noise.

IT WILL BE ALMOST IMPOSSIBLE TO HOLD THE BABY AND OTHER THINGS AT THE SAME TIME

While you are working at home, have the baby sit in a special seat close by so he can watch, but it may not be possible to hold him while you are working.

SUDDEN CHANGE IN MUSCLE TONE

can be a real nuisance when you take your baby to the grocery store or the shopping center.

He may suddenly fall back or slide from your arms when you are busy trying to find the things you want or to pay for them.

It will help to have a stroller or a special seat.

THE SEAT IN THE SHOPPING CART WILL PROBABLY NOT HOLD THE BABY WELL ENOUGH

When he is small enough, you may be able to put the infant seat in the large basket of a shopping cart.

When the baby is older, you may need to have a stroller or walker that has a basket built into it.

YOU WILL PROBABLY BE EMBARRASSED WHEN OTHERS LOOK AND STARE AT YOUR
BABY

but try to be calm and take care of your baby as if others were not there.

Some people may not have seen a baby with special problems and they may be curious.

*Some of the people may just be looking because they are interested in children, or they
might be admiring the way you take care of your baby.*

SHOPPING IS AN IMPORTANT LEARNING TIME FOR YOUR BABY AND YOU WILL WANT
TO TAKE HIM WITH YOU WHEN YOU CAN

but if you are tired or in a hurry it may be a good idea to have someone else take care of the
baby while you shop.

THE CHILD WHO HAS FREQUENT CHANGES IN MUSCLE TONE COULD GET INTO AN
UNCOMFORTABLE OR EVEN DANGEROUS POSITION VERY QUICKLY AND
SHOULD NEVER BE LEFT ALONE IN THE CAR—EVEN FOR A FEW SECONDS

Be sure that you plan some times for taking your baby out to show him things.

You may be interested in the article:
"Don't Leave Home Without It." Michaelis, C. T. *The Exceptional Parent.* June 1978.

The article is about the things that a child can learn when taken out. But it is also about the
courage that parents must have in order to take the baby out.

THERE IS MORE ABOUT TAKING THE BABY OUT IN THE LANGUAGE SECTION OF THIS
BOOK

HOLDING THE BABY FOR BATHING WILL BE DIFFICULT
IF YOUR BABY GOES STIFF SOMETIMES AND LIMP OTHER TIMES,
IT WILL BE PARTICULARLY DIFFICULT TO BATHE HIM

A sponge or rubber mat will help to prevent the baby's slipping into the bath water.

*For most babies and mothers the bath is a fun time and wise mothers allow enough time
for the baby to enjoy splashing for awhile.*

*You will probably be so concerned about your baby's safety and your ability to hold him
in the slippery water, that the bath will not be fun for you.*

IT HELPS TO BE SURE THAT YOU HAVE ALL THE THINGS YOU NEED BEFORE YOU
PICK UP THE BABY

| Warm water | Towels | The rubber duckie |
| Soap | Clean clothes | |

You will probably want to ignore the phone if it rings during the bath.

You may want to tell your friends what time you bathe the baby so they will call at other times.

Sometimes it is easier to use a small tub. You may want to put a small tub inside the bathroom tub, or, if your baby is small, put the tub in the kitchen sink.

ANOTHER SOLUTION TO SLIPPING IS TO PUT THE BABY ON A TOWEL IN THE BATH TUB

Fold the towel over once or twice at the end of the tub away from the faucets.

Put the baby's head on the folded end of the towel.

WASH THE BABY WITH A SHOWER HEAD THAT HAS A LONG HOSE SO
YOU ARE GIVING THE BABY A SHOWER WHILE HE IS LYING DOWN

That way you can control where the water goes and the baby can't slip and get hurt.

YOUR BABY MAY DROP THINGS
WHEN HIS MUSCLE TONE CHANGES FROM STIFF TO LIMP

he will have difficulty holding onto things
EVEN THINGS LIKE TOYS AND FOOD THAT HE MAY WANT

Sometimes babies play a game of dropping things to have someone else pick them up (see Social Problems, 6).

Your baby may learn that game, too.

IT IS MORE LIKELY THAT THINGS ARE DROPPED BECAUSE THE MUSCLE TONE CHANGES

IF HE DROPS SOMETHING, PUT IT QUIETLY BACK INTO THE BABY'S HAND

Although it is natural to be angry or tired, try not to say anything to the baby about dropping the object.

Put the object back into his hand again and again without drawing attention to it.

YOUR BABY MAY SIT WELL FOR AWHILE AND THEN SUDDENLY FALL TO ONE SIDE

The baby may have had a mild seizure (see
Health Problems, 1) or his muscle tone
may have changed suddenly and
caused him to go limp or stiff.

A CHANGE IN MUSCLE TONE CAN
THROW HIM OFF BALANCE

YOUR BABY CAN LEARN TO PROTECT HIMSELF FROM FALLING BY PRAC-
TICING SIDE-SITTING WITH SUPPORT

A therapist can show you how to move him
just a little while he is side-sitting.

This way he can learn to know how it feels to
almost fall and can learn what to do
about almost falling.

It is natural for you to want to protect your baby from falling and getting hurt.

BUT THE ONLY WAY A BABY CAN LEARN HOW NOT TO FALL IS TO BE ALLOWED TO
EXPLORE AND LEARN HOW IT FEELS TO ALMOST FALL AND WHAT TO DO
ABOUT THAT FEELING

IT IS IMPORTANT THAT YOUR BABY PRACTICE SITTING IN A SPACE THAT IS SAFE

Find a place where there is no furniture or other objects that the baby might bump against if he
falls.

The floor is a good place for him to practice sitting.

IT IS NOT WISE TO HAVE THE BABY PRACTICE SITTING ON A BED

The surface of a bed is not firm enough for the child to sit well and if he falls it might be a long
fall.

A RUG OR A FLOOR MAT IS THE BEST PLACE FOR THE BABY TO LEARN TO SIT

You can make a floor mat by covering a piece of foam rubber about 4' x 6' x 2" with two beach towels or a large piece of terry cloth.

If you put a zipper in one end of the cover, you can take it off and wash it.

IF THE BABY FALLS ONTO THE MAT, HE WILL NOT BE HURT

WHEN MUSCLE TONE CHANGES, YOUR BABY WILL HAVE A HARD TIME
    LEARNING TO USE THE TOILET

IT WILL BE DIFFICULT FOR THE BABY TO
    LEARN TO CONTROL THE MUSCLES OF ELIMINATION

                if his muscles are changing from stiff to limp without his control.

It will also be difficult for him to learn to sit on the toilet.

IT IS NOT POSSIBLE FOR HIM TO LEARN TO ELIMINATE ON THE TOILET
    IF HE IS AFRAID HE MIGHT FALL

If your baby is ready to be toilet-trained (and if you are ready to train him) (see Self-Help Problems, 2)

IT WILL BE NECESSARY FOR YOU TO HAVE A POTTY CHAIR OR A TOILET SEAT FOR
    THE BIG TOILET THAT WILL HOLD THE BABY CORRECTLY

A therapist can help you find one or design one for you.

SOME BABIES KEEP THEIR MOUTHS OPEN A LOT
    IT CAN BE OPEN BECAUSE THE MUSCLES ARE STIFF
    IT CAN BE OPEN BECAUSE THE MUSCLES ARE LIMP

Some babies have their mouths open **when they are excited** and are trying hard to move some other part of the body.

        Sometimes babies have their mouths open because they **want to explore** something by putting it in their mouth.

                Sometimes babies open their mouths **when they are bored or do not understand** what is happening or know what they should be doing.

WHEN THE MOUTH IS OPEN FOR A FEW SECONDS SALIVA DRIPS OUT;
  PEOPLE OFTEN CALL THIS "DROOLING"

Actually, it isn't that the baby has more saliva
  It is just that he isn't swallowing it.

*Of course you feel uncomfortable when your baby has his mouth open because he will
  not look pretty that way.*

If saliva is dripping from his mouth, he may look offensive to other people—and even to you,
  especially if he is drooling and has a runny nose.

IT WILL NOT HELP HIM TO HAVE YOU KEEP REMINDING
  OR FOR YOU TO GENTLY SLAP HIS FACE

          THE BABY NEEDS TO HAVE SOME TREATMENT TO HELP LEARN
          TO FEEL THE MUSCLES OF THE MOUTH AREA

and some practice chewing food and other things so he can learn to close his mouth
and swallow.

A therapist can show you how to help "de-
  sensitize" the inside and outside of the
  mouth (see page 25).

          YOU CAN LEARN HOW TO APPLY PRES-
          SURE AROUND THE BABY'S MOUTH

                      You can help him learn to know when his
                      mouth is open and how to close it.

                      But while he is still learning be sure that you

          KEEP HIS NECK AND CHEST DRY

                      by using thick bibs or changing his shirt
                      frequently.

5 SOME BABIES SEEM TO BE MOVING ALL THE TIME

SOME BABIES MOVE AND TWITCH WHENEVER THEY ARE AWAKE

AND SOME BABIES SEEM TO BE MOVING EVEN WHEN THEY ARE ASLEEP

When there are things to see and things to hear and things to do all at once, a person has to decide which things to watch and which things to listen to and which things to touch.

When a baby is very young he makes this decision by
Looking at the brightest thing
Listening to the loudest thing
And touching the closest thing

THE BABY PAYS SO MUCH ATTENTION TO THE STRONGEST
THING THAT HE DOESN'T SEE THE OTHER THINGS

THE BABY ONLY SEES WHAT HE WANTS TO SEE
AND HEARS WHAT HE WANTS TO HEAR
AND TOUCHES WHAT HE WANTS TO TOUCH

SOME PEOPLE HAVE TROUBLE PAYING ATTENTION TO ONE THING AT A TIME

Some babies have trouble because they
want to see everything
want to hear everything
want to touch everything
all at the same time.

In the confusion of trying to do it all, the baby
just fumbles from place to place and
from one interesting thing to another
without really enjoying any of them.

THE BABY MOVES SO MUCH AND IS SO
ACTIVE THAT HE IS CALLED HYPER
(OVER) ACTIVE

Other babies seem to be moving all the time

BECAUSE THEY DO NOT KNOW WHAT
THEY WANT TO SEE, HEAR, AND
TOUCH

They have trouble making their bodies move
effectively.

They are continually trying to get the body in
the best place to see, hear and touch
what is interesting to them.

In both kinds of movement the problem is that the baby is
not able to concentrate on one thing at a time
and get the body ready to deal with that one thing.

Of course all babies play with things on tables and things on the floors.

BUT SPECIAL BABIES SEEM TO BUMP INTO TABLES

and run into walls
handle the newspaper
and hang on the drapes

WITHOUT SEEMING TO KNOW WHAT THEY ARE DOING OR WHY THEY ARE DOING IT

If your child is always moving and touching
things it will be difficult for you or anyone
else to take care of him.

*You will probably feel embarrassed or even
hurt that your baby seems to spoil
your things and other people's things.*

*But he is not purposely trying to be a nui-
sance or purposely trying to break
things.*

*Your baby is only exploring and learning—
he needs some help in learning how
to explore.*

The first important thing that you can do is to

PUT AWAY THINGS THAT ARE VALUABLE, THINGS THAT MIGHT BREAK, AND THINGS
THAT MIGHT HURT THE BABY

Then arrange the furniture so there is as
much open space for movement as
possible.

Create some places close to the kitchen or
the utility room

WHERE THE BABY CAN BUMP INTO
THINGS AND TOUCH THINGS WITH-
OUT HURTING THE THINGS OR HIM-
SELF.

You can then allow the baby to move about
without being overly concerned about
the baby or the house being destroyed.

*Without your attractive things on display, the rooms may look bare but eventually your
baby will learn more controlled movement and you will have intact, attractive things
to use.*

IF YOU TAKE YOUR BABY TO SOMEONE'S HOUSE, THE BABY WILL PROBABLY TOUCH
THINGS AND MAYBE EVEN BREAK SOMETHING

or he may wander around the house and
open closets or play with dishes or other
things he can reach.

THIS COULD BE EMBARRASSING FOR YOU AND THE HOSTESS

It may be a house where you have been welcome for years but you may find that suddenly you
are **no longer welcome if you bring the baby.**

*Although this will probably make you un-
happy, it is never wise to take the baby
to a house where the baby is not welcome, even if the home is of a relative
or a close friend.*

Some people who have not been around children for some time (or ever) may find that even a
baby who isn't moving all the time **a disturbance.**

BUT A BABY WHO IS MOVING ALL THE TIME CAN BE DISTRESSING TO MANY PEOPLE

If you want to keep a friendship, try not to feel hurt and see your friend when you can have
someone else taking care of the baby.

Parents of special babies find that some or the old friends have trouble accepting and being around a special baby.

The parents may decide later that perhaps certain friends aren't as close as they thought.

Most parents find that when they are busy with a baby, there is less time for old friends.

BABIES WHO MOVE ALL THE TIME ARE HARD TO DRESS, BATHE, AND FEED

THEY ALSO CLIMB OUT OF BED AND ON
TOP OF FURNITURE

You will need to deal with these situations.

THE BABY IS NOT PURPOSELY TRYING TO BE DIFFICULT

He needs help to **organize the central nervous system** so he can pay attention to what he wants to pay attention to and so he can move like other babies.

A THERAPIST UNDERSTANDS HOW THE BODY MOVES

A THERAPIST CAN WATCH THE BABY'S MOVEMENTS AND DETERMINE JUST EX-ACTLY WHAT MOVEMENTS ARE DIFFICULT FOR HIM

The baby may stand up but not have learned
to balance well.

He will probably need to spend time practicing balance while sitting before trying to
balance standing up.

THE THERAPIST WILL LOOK TO SEE THE WAY THE BABY MOVES NOT JUST WHERE HE MOVES

SINCE THERAPISTS HAVE WORKED WITH MANY BABIES AND STUDIED THEIR MOVE-MENT, THEY CAN EVALUATE AND COMPARE YOUR CHILD'S MOVEMENTS TO THE NORMAL DEVELOPMENTAL SEQUENCE.

EATING SUGAR CAN CAUSE THE BABY TO BE RESTLESS AND MOVING ALL THE TIME

So can certain chemical and food preservatives.

FOR SOME CHILDREN THE REACTION IS MUCH STRONGER THAN FOR OTHERS

The foods that the body eats are converted into blood sugar. When the level is low the baby will be restless or listless. In order to keep the level even, the baby needs to eat frequently and to avoid eating foods that contain refined sugar. Foods with refined sugar in them cause the blood sugar to rise and fall rapidly.

You may be interested in the books listed on page 35. Smith's books discuss sugar and white flour which digests like sugar.

ALTHOUGH YOU MAY FEEL THAT YOUR CHILD WILL BE MISSING SOMETHING IF YOU DENY HIM CANDY,

and it might mean a major reorganization of the household to have nutritious foods for your baby, it may also make it possible to reorganize your child's behavior—for the better.

Smith suggests foods that babies and children can use for snacks instead of punch and cookies or potato chips (see page 35).

As Smith suggests in his book—

CAREFUL FEEDING, EVEN FOR ADULTS, CAN INCREASE THE ABILITY TO RESPOND TO INFECTIONS AND OTHER STRESS

6 SOME BABIES HAVE TROUBLE MAKING THEIR BODIES DO WHAT THEY WANT

Babies learn how to move the body the way they want to **by crawling under things and climbing on top of things and holding onto things and walking around things.**

After a child has "practiced" crawling under the table or around the chair a few times, his central nervous system and his body have learned to work together.

The baby knows how to make his body do what he wants it to do. Then he can make that movement over and over again smoothly without making unnecessary or awkward movements.

THE CENTRAL NERVOUS SYSTEM IN SPECIAL BABIES MAY HAVE TROUBLE BEING ABLE TO STORE THE INFORMATION ABOUT MOVING

> If the information is not stored in the central nervous system already, the child will have to make practice trial and error movements over and over again, even though he is not getting what he wants.

THE BABY WILL NOT BE ABLE TO DO WHAT HE WANTS TO DO

He will not be able to see dangers or stop moving before he is close to the harm.

THE BABY WILL LOOK CLUMSY AND DISORGANIZED

Sometimes the child will want to move or get a toy or reach some food and instead of a purposeful movement

THE BABY'S BODY WILL KEEP MOVING IN THE SAME WAY OVER AND OVER AGAIN

This is sometimes called reflex movement because it is not what the baby was choosing but it is what the body keeps repeating **regardless of what movement the baby may have been wanting to make.**

> *Although parents sometimes complain about the baby getting into everything, you will probably feel very bad if your baby is not able to move well enough to do this,*
>
> *or if he looks awkard when he tries to get into things.*

Some special babies learn to get around by lying on the tummy, lifting their head and shoulders up, reaching out with their arms, and dragging their feet and legs behind them.

Others may move around by rolling over and over again, or by sitting up and scooting along on the bottom.

If your child moves in one of these different ways

IT IS BECAUSE HE NEEDS HELP TO LEARN TO MOVE PROPERLY

Other people will probably notice and make comments about how "funny" the baby looks.

Of course you will feel uncomfortable and you may want to keep other people from seeing your baby do these things.

You may feel like holding your baby when other people are around, especially if you don't know them

or if you know that they will laugh at your baby

or try to give you advice!

REFLEX PATTERNS CONTROL THE BABY'S MOVEMENT

The reflex patterns (see page 85) make the child move the same way again and again

The reflex patterns keep him from moving to get things and do things

They make the baby look clumsy and bump into things

And they make him hard to hold and care for.

In order to **reorganize a damaged or dysfunctioning central nervous sytem so the baby can move the way he wants to move**

THE BABY WILL NEED HELP

A therapist who has had training and experience working with babies can show you what movements will help your baby.

Sometimes teachers who have worked with a therapist can show you.

THE BABY NEEDS TO ACTIVELY PARTICIPATE IN THE MOVEMENT—NOT JUST HAVE OTHERS MOVE HIS ARMS, LEGS, AND OTHER BODY PARTS.

IT IS IMPORTANT THAT YOUR BABY GET HELP TO LEARN TO MOVE MORE NATURALLY WHILE HE IS STILL YOUNG

When the baby is young, it is possible to help the system learn to do many things.

As he gets older, the system no longer is able to do new things and the reflex movements may be the only movements that the older child can make.

Before the baby learns to control the movement of the parts of the body separately

SOME PARTS OF THE BODY MOVE TOGETHER AUTOMATICALLY

These groups of automatic movements are called reflex patterns.

If the infant doesn't learn to control the movement of the parts of the body automatically, **the reflex patterns continue** and the baby will not be able to create functional movement. Every time he tries to move the same stiff movements will be repeated over and over again.

One of the things that a therapist can do to keep the baby's reflex movement from controlling his body is to

HELP HIM LEARN TO CONTROL THE PARTS OF THE BODY SEPARATELY

THE FIRST PART OF THE BODY THAT A BABY CAN LEARN TO CONTROL IS THE HEAD

The infant first learns to hold the head up and turn it.

Then he learns to control the shoulders and arms;
    then the hips;
    then the legs;
    then the feet.

At the same time that the baby is learning to control the body from the head to the feet

HE IS ALSO DEVELOPING
FROM THE CENTER TO THE EXTREMITIES

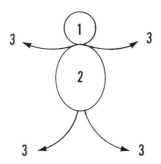

So the trunk develops before the arms, hands, and fingers and before the legs, feet, and toes.

THE BABY LEARNS TO TWIST THE TRUNK BEFORE HE LEARNS TO CONTROL THE HANDS AND FEET

TO HELP YOUR BABY LEARN TO MOVE THE PARTS OF THE BODY NATURALLY, THE THERAPIST WILL HELP HIM LEARN TO CONTROL THE PARTS IN THE ORDER THAT THEY NORMALLY DEVELOP

YOUR BABY WILL NOT BE READY TO LEARN TO CONTROL THE HIPS AND LEGS

until he has learned good control of the head and shoulders.

YOUR BABY WILL NOT BE READY TO LEARN TO MOVE THE HANDS AND FEET

until he has learned to move the hips and shoulders separately.

YOUR BABY WILL NOT BE READY TO LEARN TO TURN OVER

until he can learn to move the head, hips, and shoulders separately.

To help the baby learn to control the head the therapist may lay him on his tummy on a large ball and then move the ball slowly so the baby

will feel like moving the head and can move it without having to hold up another part of the body.

The therapist may also help the baby roll to help him learn to turn the head.

The therapist may help the baby learn to move the hips and shoulders separately by putting the baby in side-lying position (see page 60), then holding the shoulders still and moving the hips then holding the hips still and moving the shoulders.

The baby must learn to move the hips and shoulders separatly before he can turn over. Learning to turn over is the beginning of learning to sit up.

Of course it is natural for you to want your baby to learn to sit up and to walk early, but he must learn to move the hips and shoulders separately before he will be able to sit up and walk.

NO TWO PEOPLE ARE EXACTLY ALIKE IN THE WAY THAT THEY MOVE

and each body moves in a slightly different way.

The movement problems that your baby has will not be exactly like the movement problems of any other baby.

In order to understand what your baby needs.

YOU WILL NEED TO HAVE A TRAINED THERAPIST
Look at your baby
Touch your baby
Carefully watch your baby

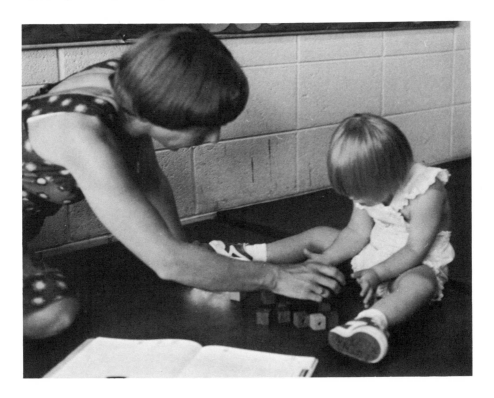

The therapist will then decide

EXACTLY WHAT YOUR BABY NEEDS

The therapist will look at the way that your baby holds the head
the therapist will look at the amount of control the baby has in the neck and shoulders
the therapist will look to see how well the baby can turn the trunk
the therapist will see how well the baby can use the mouth

THEN THE THERAPIST WILL TRY DIFFERENT KINDS OF TREATMENT

And choose some activities that are particularly good for your baby.

It is not wise to put your baby in a therapy class where all the babies are getting the same activities.

A therapy class is a little like taking one bottle of medicine and giving all sick children a dose.

Movement problems are such individual problems that you will want a

SKILLED PERSON TO EVALUATE YOUR BABY'S INDIVIDUAL PROBLEM

That person can then show you and others just exactly what to do.

It is difficult to handle the child just right so be sure that the therapist shows both parents and any grandparents, baby sitters, or siblings that might be handling the baby.

After the therapist shows you and tells you you try to do it while the therapist is still there to see if you are doing it right.

You will be tired and discouraged from time to time when you must spend extra time helping your baby learn to move. It will make bathing, feeding, and caring for the baby slow. It is natural to become tired and discouraged. Arrange something nice for yourself: a trip to the zoo; a novel from the library; (most libraries have records, too); a long distance call to an old friend; or a trip to the beauty parlor; or maybe even a lazy bubble bath.

When you come back to the baby you will feel refreshed. It is important that the movement treatment be given consistently, *and that it be given while the baby is young and still developing. So keep planning nice things for yourself.*

Some of the things that your baby does that look clumsy and awkward are really symptoms that he cannot move the parts of the body separately and the movement is still being controlled by reflexes.

IF YOUR BABY DOESN'T

> Turn over,
> crawl,
> or sit up
> and he always gets stuck between furniture and under things or slides on his bottom rather than crawling, it may be because he cannot move the parts of the body separately.

BABIES DON'T OUTGROW CLUMSINESS AND AWKWARDNESS

Actually it gets worse as they get older, because the body grows and it is harder to learn to control a larger body.

As babies grow and explore they not only learn how to get into things **they also learn how to get out of things** and they usually don't get stuck or look awkward.

It is natural for you to want to put off thinking about the baby's problems because thinking about them is discouraging and depressing and sometimes it is hard to enjoy taking care of the baby if you think about problems often.

However, when it comes to movement problems it is important that you do not accept the answer that the baby will "outgrow it."

The body can learn to be flexible and move properly only when it is young and the muscles and nerves are pliable and still developing.

The younger your baby is when you get help with the movement problems, the more he will be able to learn.

IF YOU WAIT, IT MAY BE THAT EVEN THE MOST INTENSIVE THERAPY WILL HAVE LITTLE EFFECT

7 SOMETIMES ARMS AND LEGS DON'T DO WHAT THEY SHOULD DO

It is important that a therapist or someone who has had broad experience with motor development help you so you will be sure that the real problem is with the arms and legs.

It may be that the baby hasn't learned to control the head and trunk well

BUT IT IS EASIER TO NOTICE THE PROBLEMS IN THE ARMS AND LEGS

The real problem is not the arms and legs themselves, but the head and trunk of the baby.

YOU MUST FIRST DEAL WITH THE THINGS THAT MOST BABIES LEARN FIRST

There are some babies

WHO DO NOT HAVE PROBLEMS WITH THE TRUNK OF THE BODY

but with the arms, hands, legs and feet only.

If your child's feet turn out, or if they turn in too far have someone look closely to be sure where the problem is. It may be the ankle, knee, or the hip. It is possible to put on a brace when the baby is very young to help the leg and foot grow straight. You have problably seen babies with shoes that have a bar holding the shoes apart. Although this may look awkward and uncomfortable it really doesn't bother the child as much as it might seem.

Remember that when the baby is young he learns to move the head, shoulders, trunk, and hips before he is able to use the legs (except to play with and to kick).

THE BABY DOESN'T MISS THE MOVEMENT OF THE FEET WHEN HE IS SMALL

If you wait until the **child is older** and his feet have been growing the wrong way, the baby may be ready to start using the feet.

HAVING A BRACE ON THEN IS A REAL NUISANCE

It is usually necessary for the child to sleep in the shoes and brace. Sometimes the baby is put into a cast.

Although your child may react differently the first few nights, try to be natural and calm and do not take the shoes and braces off.

After a few nights most babies sleep their usual pattern and so do their parents!

OCCASIONALLY SURGERY IS NECESSARY

Sometimes the baby is not able to move the arms and legs because the
muscles and tendons are not long enough to allow the joint to move
or they are holding the joint in an awkward position.

Surgery or bracing can sometimes help.

THERAPISTS SOMETIMES PUT ON A MOLDED PLASTIC BRACE CALLED A SPLINT

Surgery of course is individually planned.
So is bracing and splinting.

If your doctor or therapist suggests such treatment you may want to take your baby for a second opinion.

Surgery usually makes a permanent change in the baby's body. Sometimes the same effect can be developed through therapy.

Certain professionals are trained to treat problems in certain ways.

You are more likely to have surgery or bracing recommended by a doctor and therapy and splinting from a therapist

DECIDING EXACTLY WHAT TO DO FOR YOUR BABY IS SOMETIMES A VERY DIFFICULT PROBLEM

You can talk to other parents but
the problems that your baby has are not exactly like the problems that any other baby has.

Although it will be upsetting to even think about surgery or therapy for your baby try to be calm and listen carefully to the explanation that the doctor or the therapist gives you.

Ask questions. Ask to see some diagrams. Have the therapist touch and move the part of the body that the baby has trouble with. Have the professional show you the difference on the body of a child who does not have the problem.

See the section about going for an evaluation (page 99). Have someone go with you to help you listen and ask questions.

Set aside as much of your regular work as possible and make sure that you get plenty of rest and eat well. It is more difficult to make a decision if you are tired and discouraged.

*If you feel like you need it, **ask for more time to think it over**. Find some medical books and read about the problem*

But don't use the time as an excuse to do nothing.

YOU CAN LEARN TO DEAL WITH IT

MANY OTHER PARENTS HAVE LEARNED TO FACE IT

If your baby needs surgery, take someone with you to sit in the waiting room.

If you have other children who can understand, explain it to them and be sure that someone who knows and likes them is taking care of them while you are busy with the baby.

SOMETIMES WHEN THE BABY STANDS HE SEEMS TO BE PUTTING MOST OF THE WEIGHT ON ONE LEG

It is important to know exactly why the baby is doing this.
It may be that one leg is shorter than the other.
It may be that the bone in the baby's leg is not fitting
    properly into the hip socket.
It may be that the muscles in the baby's leg are short and stiff.
It may be that the baby 's spinal column is growing curved
    rather than straight.

ANY ONE OF THESE THINGS COULD MAKE THE BABY SEEM TO BE STANDING LOPSIDED

Each of the situations would need a different treatment. The baby may need:
A special shoe to hold the foot in place
Treatment to develop the hip joint
Treatment to loosen the stiff muscles in the leg
Treatment for the curve in the spine

If the problem is caused by a combination of things the baby will need a combination of treatments.

SOMETIMES A BABY'S BACK IS NOT STRAIGHT

The back bone is actually many small bones

If the baby cannot move the body easily, the
    muscles on one side pull more than the
    other side and he will begin to lean to
    that side, even when lying down.

**If this happens, the small bones of the back
will not grow to be exactly on top of
each other.** They will grow sloped toward the side just a little and there will be
a curve from side-to-side.

If the baby's body is weak on one side, it is
easy for the spine to curve toward that
side.

In order to help the spine grow straighter the
baby needs help in using both sides of
the body and learning to rotate the
trunk.

A THERAPIST CAN SHOW YOU HOW TO DO THIS

If you notice that the baby's body is bigger on one side than the other or that the shoulder leans
to one side, he needs help to keep the spine from growing crooked. If the spine grows
crooked it is called scoliosis

Of course you will feel bad if scoliosis starts to happen to your child and you will probably go off somewhere and cry.

You may want to keep your baby in clothes that cover the back and shoulders so people won't ask questions.

But be sure that you don't cover up the body and forget about it.

It is possible to prevent much of the curve, but you will have to work carefully on the trunk rotation exercises several times a day.

SOME BABIES HAVE TROUBLE HOLDING THINGS

If you put toys or food even close to most babies they pick them up.

Your baby may not be able to do this. For some babies it is hard to keep hold of things—even when they are put into the hands.

Some babies take hold of things and don't let them go.

This can be very discouraging or even embarrassing to you.

Many parents brag because the baby can hold the bottle or throw the ball.

Your baby may have trouble learning to do these things.

The trouble may be just in the baby's hands but it is more likely that the trouble with the hands is more visible than the trouble with the rest of the body.

HAVE A THERAPIST OR A TEACHER WHO IS FAMILIAR WITH EARLY MOTOR DEVELOPMENT

look at your baby carefully.

It may be that he has not learned to move the head, shoulders, and trunk (see page 85).

IF THE BABY HAS NOT LEARNED TO CONTROL THE TRUNK

and balance in sitting

IT IS DIFFICULT FOR THE HANDS AND ARMS TO BE USEFUL

for anything else because the hands and arms are needed to help maintain balance.

If the hands are still needed for balance, then they are not free to learn functional hand movements.

Sometimes therapists and teachers put a child on a wedge so he can use the hands some even though he cannot control the trunk.

You will be discouraged if the therapist tells you that the baby is **not developmentally ready to use the hands** *and you may want to have a long walk or buy a new hat to help you feel better.*

But remember that it may be that for good use of the hands your baby must have good development of the head, shoulders and trunk. Your baby's hands may develop sooner if the therapy is directed to the head, shoulders, and trunk first—and then to the hands.

8 SOME BABIES DON'T LIKE TO BE HELD AND TOUCHED

THERAPISTS MIGHT CALL THIS BEING OVERSENSITIVE

TEACHERS MIGHT CALL THIS BEING WITHDRAWN OR AUTISTIC

Grandmothers, grandfathers, aunts, uncles, and friends like to hold babies and play with them. Even politicians chuck babies under the chin and kiss them.

And most babies smile and coo back.

BUT SOME BABIES DON'T LIKE TO BE TOUCHED AND CUDDLED

>   **They go stiff and pull away**

*If your baby doesn't smile and coo when someone touches him, you will probably be uncomfortable. And you will be even more uncomfortable if the baby doesn't smile and coo when **you** touch him.*

SMILING AND COOING ARE PARTLY SOMETHING THAT BABIES LIKE TO DO WHEN THEY ARE FIRST BORN AND PARTLY SOMETHING THAT BABIES MUST LEARN TO DO

Liking to be touched and talked to

>   **can begin even in the delivery room when you hold and talk to the baby.**

>   Even at that time the baby
>   **can respond by looking back at the face of the person who is talking.**

If your baby was born premature or with some problems or if it was a difficult birth,

>   **it may not have been possible to hold and touch and talk to your baby when he was only minutes old.**

If he doesn't learn to like to be touched when very young,
>   then when he is touched, he will be startled or frightened—
>   a little like you might feel if someone came up behind you and touched you when you didn't know that they were there.

HELPING THE BABY LIKE TO BE TOUCHED MAY BE A SLOW PROCESS

>   Learning to like anything new takes time.
>   It may take time for your baby to learn to like to be touched.

It must be a gradual process that is repeated day after day, not something that happens all at once.

For some babies being touched feels a little like being tickled and it is uncomfortable to them.

The baby's central nervous system is so sensitive that it makes a strong response to even little messages.

It will help the baby be comfortable when being touched, if you can be comfortable while you are doing the touching.

It is natural to feel uncomfortable when you are taking care of a baby for the first time or when you are taking care of a baby that is fragile or has special problems.

But if you touch and hold the baby gingerly because you are afraid that you will hurt him,

the baby will feel the uncertainty of the touch and will respond not by relaxing and being comfortable, but by becoming tense.

It is difficult to keep touching when your baby doesn't respond, but keep touching. Your baby needs more, not less touching.

HOLD THE BABY FIRMLY

Back packs and infant seats are not good places to keep a baby that is sensitive to touch.

The baby needs to feel the soft warmth of your body not the pressure of the denim bag or the rigidness of an infant seat.

It is important to help the baby learn to like to be touched **when he is still small enough to hold**

It will be much more difficult to teach him to enjoy being touched when he is bigger.

The baby will also have lost many **social opportunities**

if he does not cuddle and respond when someone touches and talks to him.

These social exchanges are the beginning of language (see Language Problems, page 135).

When you hold the baby who doesn't like to be held,

HOLD HIM FIRMLY AGAINST YOUR BODY

> so he can feel the pressure of your touch and the pressure of your body.

If you touch the baby lightly, the sensitive central nervous system will send many light sensations that will be frustrating rather than comfortable to him.

In order to keep him from feeling that he is being tickled, hold him against your body **rather than in your hands**.

BABIES WHO ARE STIFF AND CAN'T BEND THE JOINTS DON'T LIKE TO BE HELD

> **and it is difficult to hold them**

YET IT IS IMPORTANT FOR BABIES TO HAVE THE FEELING OF BEING HELD

It may be helpful to have a therapist show you some of the ways that you could handle the baby.

Some of the ways are described in a book that tells parents to hold the baby against the parent's body and to be sure that the baby's knees are bent.

The book also shows how to bathe the baby and how to make the baby comfortable in play.

The book is *Handling the Young Cerebral Palsied Child at Home* by N. Finnie, E. P. Dutton and Company, New York, 1975.

BABIES WHO HAVE HEALTH PROBLEMS SOMETIMES DO NOT LIKE TO BE HELD

> **and you may be uncomfortable about how much movement is good for them**

Since touching and moving is such an important part of development your baby needs to be moved and touched **as much as possible**.

In order for your therapist to help you know **exactly** how much movement is good for the baby it would be a good idea to arrange that you and the therapist meet with the doctor to talk together about what kinds of touching and moving would be good for the baby.

> **Sometimes doctors are not aware of the new treatment therapists can give and sometimes therapists are not aware of medical complications.**

Rather than guess or have your baby miss something, it would be a good idea to discuss the plan of therapy together.

Doctors and therapists are busy and it may be difficult for you to arrange for them to be together, but it will be worth the effort to make those arrangements.

It would be a good idea for both parents to go, if possible. Since it will be a trying experience for you, be sure that you take someone along to help you drive and take care of the baby and talk to the therapist and doctor.

Of course you won't feel this is an ordinary trip to the doctor and you may need to spend some time getting used to the idea. Try to do that before or after you see the doctor and therapist so you can learn as much as possible during the visit. If you try, you can make yourself "hold up" during the visit. Plan to allow yourself time to unwind later.

When you schedule the appointment, be sure that you tell the receptionist that you need time for discussion and questions or you may be frustrated because there is not enough time to ask about all the things that you want to know.

If your baby doesn't like to

be bounced on the knee
be tossed in the air
have his teeth brushed
have his face washed
have his nose wiped

it may be that the baby is oversensitive and **needs to be desensitized** (see page 25).

If your baby scratches or hits himself, it may also be that the feeling of being touched is not a comfortable feeling and **the baby needs to get used to being handled** (see page 3).

Most of the things that a baby learns during the first year are things that you can see him doing.

He learns to use the body and to move the body.

If he is not able to learn to use the body, it is probable that the baby will have other problems since

most learning is dependent on being able to move the body in order to see and participate.

More complicated movement is dependent on the development of simple movement. It is important that you help your baby learn the simple movement now so he can learn the more complicated movement later.

YOUR BABY CAN NOT LEARN A "HIGHER" SKILL UNTIL THE "LOWER" SKILL IS
LEARNED

Thus, your baby may be older than a year, but still need to be working on skills that most
babies learn during the first year.

V

You May Be Concerned About Social Problems and Questions

1   SOME BABIES DON'T LIKE TO BE AROUND OTHER PEOPLE

A teacher or a psychologist would call the
baby *unresponsive*.

For most babies and for most adults **being
with other people is pleasant.**

It **is a time to smile and talk and touch and
enjoy one another's company.**

Most babies let you know when they are
awake. They either cry or make loud
cooing noises.

**Some special babies don't let you know
when they are awake.** They simply lie
quietly and gaze at the ceiling.

Some babies don't seem to enjoy associating
with others.

THEY SEEM ALWAYS TO WANT TO BE ALONE

SOME SPECIAL BABIES DON'T SMILE WHEN YOU TALK TO THEM

Some don't reach out to be touched or held.

The baby may be
extra sensitive to touch

and need to have careful touching
and holding to get used to being
touched (see Motor Problems, 7).

Or he may need to have you touch and smile
longer in order for him

**to be able to understand what is hap-
pening and to get a response ready.**

Sometimes special babies are

GETTING READY TO SMILE

and the adults turn away because

THEY EXPECT THE SMILE SOONER

IT IS VERY DIFFICULT TO KEEP SMILING WHEN A BABY IS NOT SMILING BACK AT YOU

You may feel ridiculous or hurt.

When an adult does not answer, you stop talking.

When a baby doesn't coo or like to be held, it is natural to feel rejected and want to turn away.

Many special babies are not able to respond
quickly, even if they want to.

**The central nervous system may be slow in
sending messages**

or the central nervous system may send
incorrect messages.

**The baby may also have trouble learning and
must hear and see the same thing
many times**

before he understands the meaning.

So in order to help the special baby learn to
smile and coo

THE SPECIAL BABY NEEDS TO BE
SMILED AND COOED TO MORE
THAN OTHER BABIES

The special baby won't do this; he is likely to simply look back at you or he may turn away when you coo and smile at him.

You will feel the baby is not interested in playing with you and it will be natural to not want to play with him or talk to him when he does not respond or turns away.

But it is important that

INSTEAD OF PLAYING AND TALKING LESS, YOU PLAY AND TALK MORE

**Your special baby will need experiences that
help him learn to be around other people,** just as other babies do.

You may need to make a special effort

>to see that your baby has enough social
experience to learn from other people.

>>You will probably need to continue the expe-
riences longer and see that they happen
oftener

>>>so he has enough time to learn.

There are several books that tell

HOW BABIES LEARN FROM BEING AROUND THE ADULTS IN THEIR WORLD

They describe the way babies develop ways of communication with others and begin to be
"social."

Some good books on communication are:

Trotter, S., and Thoman, E. B. *Social Responsiveness of Infants*, Johnson and Johnson
Baby Products, 1978.
Describes how babies start learning language by communication with smiles and coos and
eye contact even when he is newborn.

Chance, P. C. *Learning Through Play*, Garner Press, New York, 1979.
Tells how the baby learns to handle objects and people through spontaneous play.

Lewis, D. *The Secret Language of Your Child*, Berkley Publishing, New York, 1978.
Tells how babies and children communicate with body language.

Brazelton, T. B. *Infants and Mothers*, Dell Publishers, New York, 1969.
Describes how babies have different personalities.

Brazelton, T. B. *Toddlers and Families*, Dell Publishers, New York, 1974.
Describes how the growing child learns to show others what he wants and needs.

If babies don't learn how to
SMILE AND COO AND USE BODY LANGUAGE
to get what they want

THEY MAY USE OTHER SIGNALS TO GET THE
attention they need
They may:
pull on skirts or pants
kick shins or hit the face of the person
who picks them up

They may pull hair and glasses and not stop
even when you try to distract them.

ALTHOUGH THE BABY MAY BE WANTING YOU TO RESPOND AND PLAY
he may not know how to do this.

The baby may have been doing these things because he has been
unsuccessful in letting people know what he wants by cooing and smiling.

THE BABY IS NOT TRYING TO HURT YOU

or make you feel bad
He is only trying to get your attention

AND DOESN'T KNOW HOW ELSE TO DO IT

*Of course you will **feel unhappy and be embarrassed** if the baby hits you or someone else and people criticize you.*

Be calm and patient and try to help him learn another way.

You can help by watching more closely to make sure that you are giving your baby a chance to learn to communicate appropriately. Be sure that you talk and smile at him. Hold him and smile when he looks at you.

The baby will know that you really enjoy being with him.

You will need to learn to

pay attention to the smiles and try to ignore the hitting and hair pulling.

It is difficult to ignore something that is unpleasant to you

but babies learn to keep repeating things that get attention.

If you keep scolding him for things that you don't like and not paying attention to the things that you do like,

your baby will keep doing whatever it is that you seem to notice.

The book, *Teaching Social Behavior to Young Children* by W. C. Sheppard, S. B. Shank, and D. Wilson, Research Press, Champaign, IL, 1973, may help you. It tells how to handle the little situations that occur over and over again while you are taking care of a young child.

Babies who don't like to be touched or held are more likely to develop social and communication problems.

Babies learn to enjoy being around other people

by enjoying the experience of being fed, bathed, and dressed

If your baby has motor problems

and it is more difficult for you to feed, dress, and bathe him, you will probably respond by being tense

and not enjoying the baby.

IF YOU ARE TENSE THE BABY WILL NOT ENJOY THE EXPERIENCE

In order to work on the social responsiveness of the baby with movement problems, it will be necessary to work on the movement problems as well as the social problems.

If the child is limp, stiff, or sensitive to touch, a therapist can help you become comfortable enough to play the "smile and coo" game with the baby while you are taking care of him. (see Motor Problems, 1, 2, 3)

Even though you may be extremely worried about your baby's health or physical problems or uncomfortable because he has learning problems **it is important that he feel that you like him,**

JUST AS HE IS

and it is important that you

HOLD YOUR BABY AND PLAY WITH HIM

It is important that he receive from you **spontaneous warmth and acceptance**

Only then will he feel

enough confidence to want to coo and
smile at you and at other people who
talk to the baby.

Of course you may feel like crying about your baby's problems from time to time. Do it while he is asleep or get someone else to take care of him for awhile.

Don't let the baby know that the problems upset you. *If your baby has always had problems they are natural to him.*

2 SOME BABIES ARE UNCOMFORTABLE IF MOTHER IS NOT AROUND

A teacher or a psychologist would call the baby **dependent** and perhaps label the mother as **overprotective**.

If you have a special baby, it is **easy to become an overprotective mother**.

Your baby needs care and attention to survive, just as other babies do.

But he needs more care and attention to deal with the special problems.

SOMETIMES IT IS HARD TO KNOW WHAT YOUR BABY NEEDS AND WHAT HE DOESN'T

It is very easy for a mother to want to be sure that the baby gets everything that he needs and for the mother to do too many things for him.

FATHERS ARE USUALLY NOT WITH BABIES AS MUCH AS MOTHERS

and might think that the baby needs less special care and attention than the mother thinks.

You may disagree so much about how much special care the baby needs that you argue about it.

Since both parents are interested in the baby,

it is difficult to be calm,

and it is easy to get into heated discussions about the baby's needs or to carry on a cold war of nondiscussion to avoid the uncomfortable feelings of disagreement.

It is important to know that even parents of babies with no special problems disagree about what the baby's needs are.

YOU WILL PROBABLY DISAGREE MORE, SINCE YOU HAVE MORE DECISIONS TO MAKE

Try to talk about the problems when the child is not around and then support each other in the decisions.

It is very important that the mother is not making all the decisions and providing all the care for the child.

If so, baby learns to be uncomfortable whenever he is not receiving the mother's attention.

Help your baby learn to feel comfortable, even when you are not there.

Your baby will not learn to be comfortable with others unless you give the baby some

> **experience being with others**
> of course, you wouldn't want to leave your baby with a stranger unless there is an emergency.

CHOOSE SOMEONE WITH WHOM YOU FEEL COMFORTABLE

Many parents of special babies do not feel comfortable leaving the child with a teenage babysitter.

> They often prefer leaving the baby with an older woman or someone who has had experience with special babies.

Sometimes nurses babysit and sometimes teachers take care of children. If you live in a city where there is a university, you may be able to find some students who are studying to be special education teachers who would like to take care of the baby. Student nurses sometimes take care of infants.

Since these people know a lot about child development already, it is easier to be comfortable leaving the baby with them.

You will want the baby to be around the other person while you are still home for awhile if at all possible. It would also be nice to leave the baby for a short trial run the first time. If this is not possible, have the sitter come early enough to let the baby feel comfortable. Show the sitter how to hold the baby, how to feed him and where his things are. It might be helpful to have a schedule written for the babysitter so the sitter will know when the baby usually sleeps and eats.

GRANDPARENTS OFTEN MAKE GOOD BABYSITTERS FOR SPECIAL BABIES BUT NOT ALWAYS

Sometimes grandparents are more nervous and concerned about the baby than the parents are and they might not be calm enough for you to feel comfortable when the baby is with them.

> They also may not agree with you on some of the care routines and they may handle the baby in a way that is unfamiliar to him.

IF YOU ARE NOT COMFORTABLE WITH THE GRANDPARENTS AS BABYSITTERS

then arrange for someone else to sit and explain that you thought it was easier or that you didn't want the grandparents to have to leave their home, or simply tell them that you are uncomfortable when they are taking care of the baby.

BE FIRM—AND DON'T FEEL GUILTY

You can arrange for them to see the baby when you are home with him or during a visit to their house when you will also be there.

BABY AND DADDY NEED TO SPEND SOME TIME TOGETHER

Time in which daddy is in charge

of the feeding or bathing or dressing or taking baby for a walk or a ride.

It is important for both parents that daddy is in charge of caring for baby sometimes.

It is also important for the baby.

As each person handles the child, they do it in a slightly different way.

If only mother feeds and cares for the baby, then the baby will balk when others must care for him.

This means that the **baby will be unnecessarily dependent on the mother and the mother will be unnecessarily tied to the baby.**

SOMETIMES MOTHERS ENCOURAGE THE BABY TO BE DEPENDENT

When daddy starts to feed the baby and has some problems doing it, mother takes the spoon and says

"Here, let me do it."

In this way the baby knows that all he has to do is spit out the food or fuss and he can control the mother.

This also leaves father out of the process.

It might be a good idea for daddy to plan to feed the baby regularly each night or certain nights and mother plan to do other things either around the house or some shopping or perhaps even a luxurious bubble bath or curl up with a good book.

Or it might work out better to have daddy be in charge of bathtime, or play time or, maybe some of each.

IF THE BABY BECOMES TOO DEPENDENT ON THE MOTHER

Then he will not go to sleep unless the mother stays in the room. Or he will wake up as soon as mother leaves the room (see Sleep Problems, 2). Sometimes this close dependency encourages the baby to wake up at night so the mother will hold him.

If your baby is waking up at night and wanting to be rocked, it may be that he is so used to mother's attention that he is not comfortable and cannot sleep without it.

Of course it is extremely important for the baby and the mother to be close and for the mother to take care of the baby and caress him and talk to him.

But if the closeness is so strong that other people are left out the baby will not "grow up" but will always be a dependent baby.

If your baby won't let anyone else care for him and clings when you leave, or if the baby fusses for a long time when you leave,
it doesn't mean that you made a mistake in leaving
It might mean that you should leave more often. It is important for you and the baby to know that you can get along without each other for a while.

If your baby is afraid of new places and new people, it doesn't mean that you should avoid taking the baby out or having others take care of the baby.

It means that you should gradually broaden the baby's experiences so there are less and less things that are "new" to the baby.

The article, "Don't Leave Home Without It" by C. T. Michaelis, in *The Exceptional Parent*, June 1978, describes some strategies for taking the baby out.

3 SPECIAL BABIES GET INTO THINGS, JUST AS OTHER BABIES DO—AND THEN SOME!

Babies are curious and must find out about things by touching and tasting.

Frequently they touch things that could hurt them and taste things that are **not food**. (See Feeding Problems, 3.)

You will need to watch your special baby closely—just like other babies, and then some!

Since most special children have more trouble learning to ask questions and often don't take you by the hand to show you what they are interested in—**they just explore on their own**

it is very important that the baby doesn't have access to soaps, disinfectants, plastic sheets, small objects that could get into the mouth, sharp objects, open stairways, loose rugs, and, and, and. . .

It is sometimes difficult to predict what a baby will want to play with.

Some things cannot be moved easily.

Things like
> the toilet bowl,
> the electric plugs,
> stairways,
> and heat vents.

Other things like
> wastebaskets,
> newspapers,
> ash trays,
> and houseplants

can be moved—and it is wise to do that.

Whatever is loose and will be interesting and some things that are not loose, but with persistant pulling the baby can loosen, **the baby will play with**.

The special baby is likely to take liquid soap from an open lower cupboard and drink it or pour it on the floor and finger paint or rub it into his eyes.

As he becomes able to move around more, the baby will continually find more things that are attractive.

TRY TO PUT THEM OUT OF SIGHT OR OUT OF REACH

Some people put locks on some cupboards so the baby cannot get certain things that may be harmful if they are eaten.

Your baby might:

> play in the toilet water—(and even drink it)
> open the door and go out in the street or hall
> play with the soap under the sink—even eat it
> mark the wall with magic marker or crayon
> play with the ash trays, light cords, and plugs
> dig in the dirt in the houseplants—perhaps pick off the leaves
> pull things out of the cupboard and open drawers
> empty the wastebasket on the floor
> eat newspapers

Although it will be a real nuisance to you, it is important for you to remember

THE BABY IS NOT TRYING TO BOTHER YOU

THE BABY IS TRYING TO LEARN ABOUT ALL THE THINGS THAT ARE AROUND HIM

If you take the baby to a safe place or keep him in a play pen all of the time or put him in a special room away from the family,

THE BABY WILL NOT BE LEARNING

Try to make your house as safe as possible and arrange your work so you can keep an eye on your baby while you work.

You might do this by folding diapers in the living room or having the baby play on the kitchen floor while you are doing the dishes and save things like scrubbing the floor until daddy is around to help—either by scrubbing the floor or watching the baby.

If the baby does something that is dangerous

Try not to get excited and show the excitement to the baby

The baby probably doesn't know that it is dangerous.

Calmly take the child away from the object or the object away from the child and say "No. No."

Then give the baby something that he can play with

It will probably take your baby years to learn which things he may play with and which things are to be left alone.

Of course you may get discouraged—but eventually your baby will know the difference.

In the mean time be patient and put away all your good or breakable things and make sure that the dangerous ones are carefully stored away.

Help your child learn by showing pleasure when he is playing with appropriate things.

There are some things that you will want to be sure that your baby can't reach:

> pins, buttons, and other small objects
> plastic bags
> soaps, cleaning fluids, bleach, furniture polish, waxes
> insect sprays, weed killers
> shoe polish, fingernail polish, polish remover
> make up, aftershave, toothpaste
> medications of all kinds
> guns and firearms of all kinds

It is easy for your baby to get burned in cooking areas or where there is a fireplace or heat outlet. Floor furnaces and portable heaters are especially dangerous to a baby who is crawling.

Swimming pools, wading pools, a garage with an automatic door opener, glass doors, and stairs can be dangerous places for the baby.

You will also want to keep your child safe in the car.

Baby and the whole family usually enjoy going for a ride. He needs to be protected by being in an infant carrier that is strapped in, or a safety seat or harness, or a seat belt, depending on how large the child is. A child who has cerebral palsy may need to have a special seat constructed that will be comfortable and safe. The occupational or physical therapist could help design one for you.

It is safer for your baby to be protected in his own seat than it is for you to hold him in the car. In case of a sudden stop or accident, the baby may be thrown from your arms.

The center of the back seat in a protected chair or harness is the safest place for the child to be.

4 SOME SPECIAL BABIES DON'T SEEM TO WANT TO PLAY WITH TOYS

Actually they may not be able to hold the toy or understand how it was designed to be used.

It is also possible that what the baby sees is a blotch of color rather than a well organized toy-object.

Most babies are interested in rattles, dolls and an assortment of small plastic toys. They like to hold them and shake them and chew on them.

As children get older they begin to use toys for some purpose like pushing cars on the floor or rolling a ball.

Your special baby may not do this. He may take the toy when you hand it to him but then let the toy drop or merely hold it and not look at it or play with it.

Some special babies wake up in a crib full of bright-interesting toys and lie looking at the ceiling rather than playing with the toys around them.

THE SPECIAL BABY MAY NOT MOVE TOWARD TOYS TO PICK THEM UP OR PUSH OR PULL THEM OR ENJOY INSPECTING THEM

This will be discouraging, and quite often, embarrassing when people hand the baby a toy and he is not interested. Grandparents may spend a considerable amount of time looking for an expensive toy to interest the baby and he may not even look at it.

IF THE BABY IS NOT INTERESTED IN THE TOY OR THE GADGET TRY TO UNDERSTAND THAT FOR SOME REASON THE OBJECT IS NOT APPEALING.

It might be that:

1. The toy is designed for the skills of a child older than your baby.

2. The toy is designed for the skills of a baby of the same age as yours, but your baby is not ready for the toy because he has not yet learned the skills of even younger babies.

3. The toy was not well enough designed to be interesting to any baby. (It may interest only adults.)

It is important to remember that special babies like all other babies are frequently more interested in a large cardboard box or a kitchen gadget than they are in the "commercial" toys. The child may be more likely to play with spoons while mother is doing the dishes than to play with a specially designed stacking toy.

MOST SPECIAL BABIES NEED HELP TO LEARN TO PLAY WITH TOYS

Most special babies don't set out to explore what would be fun to do. They learn best by watching what others do then trying to do it themselves.

In order for your special baby to enjoy a toy or
a box or a kitchen gadget, he needs to
see someone else having fun with it.

Then he can repeat what the other person did
with the object.

Some researchers who study play found that
if an adult crawled along pushing a truck
or played tea party by sitting and drinking the imaginary drink, **the baby learned
faster**. The child also learned to communicate and socialize with others better.

AN IMPORTANT ASPECT OF PLAY TIME IS THAT IT IS A TIME WHEN THERE IS NO
DEFINITE GOAL AND WHEN MAKING "MISTAKES" DOESN'T MATTER

The book, *Learning Through Play* by Paul Chance, Gardner Press, Inc., New York, 1979,
describes the play process and how it is related to learning.

**It is important that the child's play is di-
rected by a warm, accepting adult** and
the baby is allowed to choose the play
objects and what will be done with them.

SPECIAL BABIES NEED MORE PLAY
THAN OTHER BABIES AND THEY
NEED HELP IN KNOWING HOW TO
PLAY

THEY NEED TO HAVE THE ADULT JOIN IN
THE PLAY AND ENJOY PLAYING

They also need to play with other children
who are developmentally similar or a little ahead of them.

IF YOU DON'T ENJOY THE PLAY, IT ISN'T PLAY

and if it isn't play the activity loses the value of being a time when the child is free to experiment.

IT IS QUITE LIKELY THAT PLAYING WITH YOUR SPECIAL BABY WILL NOT BE AS MUCH FUN AS IT WOULD IF THE BABY WERE BETTER ABLE TO "PLAY ALONG" BUT IT IS IMPORTANT THAT HE FEELS THAT IT IS FUN FOR YOU

And that you are enjoying the time with him.

—that you have nothing more important to do at that particular time

—than to enjoy being with the baby and doing

—what is interesting to him.

Try to make the time pleasant for you, too by kicking off your shoes, taking the baby out in the fresh air, or turning on some of your favorite music.

It would be a good time to play some children's music, too. The Kimbo Educational records: Self Help 8055 and Socialization 8056 would be especially good playtime music. Kimbo Educational, Long Branch, NJ.

It would be good to plan several times a day when you could **regularly** play with the baby. It is usually more convenient to do this just after meals, bath, or dressing time.

If your baby knows when to expect play and that you will set other things aside for awhile, he will learn to understand and participate more quickly.

MAKE SURE THAT THE TOYS THAT YOU HAVE FOR YOUR BABY ARE DURABLE

and attractive and that they do not need to be pulled or turned or used in a way that may be difficult for him to learn.

A jack in the box, for example, is usually difficult to close and sometimes even frightening when it opens.

A singing top might interest your baby, but it would not be as interesting to him as something that he could move without help.

Balls of all sizes, stuffed toys, dolls, and objects of molded plastic make good toys for the young baby.

There are also a number of musical toys that the baby can hit to make music.

A small unbreakable mirror is an excellent toy for a special baby. He will enjoy playing with the baby that is reflected in a durable wall mirror that is floor length.

Remember to check the kitchen or housewares department of a variety store for suitable colored plastic containers that your baby might find interesting.

Your child will probably need toys that are for young babies even as he gets older. Sometimes special children need infant toys even though they are school age. If you look carefully you can find simple toys that are attractive.

Of course you want your child to have nice things and you may behave like the proud father who brings a baseball mitt to the hospital as a gift for his new son. The baby will not be ready for the baseball mitt for years, even though father is ready now.

If you want to buy some "baseball mitt" toys, think of them as gifts for yourself or decorations for the house. What the special baby needs is something to "sink his teeth into" —literally.

Although you may want to give your baby everything, it is better for him to play with a few familiar toys over and over again. If there are fewer toys, the baby will have more of a chance to become familiar with them, and will remember how to use them and the pleasure of playing with them.

ALL TOYS MUST BE STRONG ENOUGH THAT THE PIECES WON'T PULL OFF WHEN THE BABY YANKS AND CHEWS THEM

Johnson and Johnson Baby Products Company, Piscataway, NJ 08854, has developed some delightful infant toys that can be used to help special babies learn, even when they are no longer young babies.

Your baby may not agree with you about what objects you think are valuable.
He may happen to like something that doesn't even look interesting to you.

BUT IF HE LIKES IT, AND IT'S SAFE, IT IS A GOOD TOY FOR HIM

A GOOD TOY IS ONE THAT THE BABY

LIKES TO LOOK AT
LIKES TO LISTEN TO
CAN PICK UP
CAN HIT
CAN THROW
CAN PUSH
CAN PULL
CAN PUT INTO THE MOUTH

Since all babies are different, what is a good toy for one may not be even slightly interesting to another.

This is partly because some babies are ready to learn new things before others and partly because some simply like things that others do not.

YOU MAY HAVE TOYS THAT ARE JUST RIGHT FOR YOUR BABY, BUT HE MAY NOT PLAY WITH THEM—YOU MUST HELP HIM LEARN TO USE THE TOYS

Babies (and other people) learn by doing
what they see others doing.

Your baby needs to have someone show him
how to play with toys. He will need to
see it over and over again.

As babies play with toys they learn how to
think and later how to talk.

You can show your baby some things to do with toys that will help him.
Learn to like to be around other people
Learn to use words to describe what happens

The baby learns from watching you play with the toys and from trying to do many different things with the toys

Remember, to the baby "toy" is anything that interests him, not necessarily a manufactured toy.

BABIES LEARN TO WATCH AN OBJECT AND TO BE ABLE TO FIND THE OBJECT WHEN IT IS HIDDEN

At first your baby will learn to watch an object
as you move it in front of his face.

Then he will be able to find the object when
you put something over part of it, while
he is watching.

Then he can learn to find something familiar
if you cover it completely while he is
watching.

Then he can learn to find something familiar
if it is hidden in two different places while
he is watching, then three places, and so
on.

DRESSING AND BATHING ARE GOOD TIMES TO PLAY "WHERE DID THE SHOE GO?",
"WHERE IS THAT SHIRT?", OR "WHERE IS THE SOAP?"

In the beginning be sure that the baby is watching when you hide the object. Sometimes a
shoe will be hard for you to find because it has slipped under the bed or is hidden under a
shirt. These natural times are good times to help the baby learn to watch objects.

What your baby is learning is that the toy or object is a permanent object. At first the babies
think that something "disappears" or no longer exists when they cannot see it, **because
they have not learned to "remember" the object.**

That is why your baby does not want to let go of a favorite toy or blanket and cries when mother
goes away. The baby thinks that the toy or blanket or mother is gone forever when he can
no longer see it. He can learn that these things are permanent only by watching them
leave and return over and over again.

You can enjoy teching your baby that objects are permanent if you and he play a game of **hide
and seek** or **peek-a-boo** while you are taking care of the baby.

**Some babies need months and months to
be able to understand that an object is
permanent.**

*It is natural for you to wish that your baby would suddenly understand, but he will learn
slowly, as all babies do.*

*Try to relax and enjoy playing. Your baby will learn better if the play experience is relaxed
and fun for both of you.*

You can learn to enjoy the **little things** *that baby learns. As you see these things, you will learn
to see more little things,* **and you will know that your baby is making progress**.

BABIES LEARN THAT ONE THING HAPPENS BECAUSE SOMETHING ELSE HAPPENED

The baby learns that when he does one thing,
another thing will happen. For example,

he learns that when a blanket or scarf is
on his head and he pulls on the blanket
or scarf, the blanket or scarf will come
off. This is another way to play peek-a-
boo.

He learns that if a toy on a blanket is out of
reach, he can get the toy by pulling on
the blanket.

He learns that if a squeeze toy is squeezed
there will be a squeaking noise.

He learns that when he hits the crib mobile,
the little animals on the string will
"dance."

After your baby watches you pull a blanket or squeeze a toy, he will eventually try the same
thing. The baby will take the squeeze toy and push it against the wall to hear the noise,
play peek-a-boo with the bath towel, or hit the crib mobile with the teddy bear.

He will learn to do the activity for the sheer delight of having the experience.

*Your special baby might enjoy experiences like playing with the ashes in the fireplace or
the water in the toilet bowl—it will be hard to see that as a "learning experience." You
will have to remove him from the area of such activities and quickly substitute
another, equally satisfying, experience.*

After your baby learns to squeeze a toy, turn on a music box, or play peek-a-boo, **you may
become very tired of repeating the same thing over and over again.**

However, your child is doing the activity for the sheer joy of seeing **that the same thing
happens over and over again.**

*Most parents get tired of babies' repeated games and you will probably have more rea-
sons that most parents to get tired because*

It will take your baby longer to tire of the joy of learning how to control the experience.

If you play along with him and add similar experiences (a second toy to squeeze, an unbreakable mirror to play peek-a-boo with, etc., see page 123), the baby will be able to move
gradually from peek-a-boo to pull toy to tricycle, then to more complicated activities.
**Thus, it is worth listening to the squeek of a favorite toy until the baby is ready to move
on.**

Don't sit and wait. Have some other toy/object demonstrations already begun and play some
of the old games and some of the new ones.

BABIES LEARN TO DO A THING WHEN THEY CAN OBSERVE SOMEONE ELSE DOING
THAT THING

Most of the things that your baby does he saw someone else doing. Babies wave bye-bye or clap pat-a-cake because they have seen you do these things. Most babies imitate quickly.

YOUR SPECIAL BABY WILL PROBABLY NEED TO SEE ANOTHER PERSON REPEAT AN ACTION MANY TIMES BEFORE HE CAN IMITATE IT.

He will need to see you wave bye-bye or clap pat-a-cake many, many, many times before he will realize that he can do that, too.

SOMETIMES IT HELPS TO HAVE SOMEONE DEMONSTRATE THE MOVEMENT AND HAVE ANOTHER PERSON STAND BEHIND THE BABY AND HELP HIS BODY MOVE IN THE SAME WAY

BOTH BYE-BYE AND PAT-A-CAKE MOVEMENTS ARE IMPORTANT

Waving is the beginning of expressing ideas through specific movement. Linguists call this "gesture language."

Pat-a-cake is the beginning of imitating movements together with a song. It helps the baby socialize, move in rhythmic patterns, and follow instructions.

Of course it is significant for your baby to learn to wave bye-bye and play pat-a-cake but if he is not ready to sit up alone, he is not ready to use his hands in this way.

If your baby cannot hold his head up and keep his trunk balanced, he is not ready to use his hands. The section on motor development describes how the body develops from the head downward and from the trunk outward. The baby must be able to control his head and trunk enough to sit before he is ready to use his arms and hands for gestures.

Of course you will be anxious, but instead of teaching waving and clapping, you will help your baby learn better by helping him learn to hold his head up and to sit. If you push too much, it will take longer.

BABIES LEARN THAT AN OBJECT WILL DO THE SAME THING AGAIN AND AGAIN

It may take your special baby a long time to learn about objects.

A toy is not something to be looked at.
    A toy is for touching
    A toy is for moving
    A toy is for doing

Your baby could use **anything** as a toy. He
    may try to touch and move **everything**.

The toys that are most popular with young babies are toys that can be

chewed
hit
thrown

in that order

In the discussion about how the body develops there is a description of the developmental pattern. The body develops from the head downward and from the inside to the outside.

Learning to use toys follows the same pattern. The baby learns
to chew (Activity of the head)
to hit (Activity of the arm)
to throw (Activity of the arm and hand)

Other things that babies and children do with toys involve the use of the **lower part of the body—like walking with pull toys and learning to ride a tricycle.**

THAT LEARNING COMES AFTER CHEWING, HITTING, AND THROWING

It will be easy for you to become impatient with your baby, because your baby will probably need to chew, hit, and throw longer than other babies and you will get very tired of having everything chewed, hit and thrown. But try to be patient, put away your good things and get some durable toys. Arrange to spend some time with only adults. Your baby will not learn to take care of things until after he has learned to explore things.

The important thing is that the baby learns that he **can use a toy in the same way over and over again**. When he begins to use a toy the same way again and again,

HE LEARNS TO "OPERATE" THE TOY

Your special baby will need plenty of time to learn to "operate" a toy **and he will need toys that operate easily**. (For a discussion of what toys would be helpful, see pages 117-119).

Sometimes special children want to use a
half-broken toy for years and years.

Occasionally they will accept a new toy like
the old one, but chances are that what
they like are the rough edges and faded
colors of the old toy.

You will naturally feel uncomfortable taking the "broken toy" when you take your baby out. You may be afraid that others will think you are neglecting your baby by giving

him old toys. Some people who don't understand children may think that—they may even say something to you. Try to ignore this. Everyone has a favorite pair of old shoes or fishing hat or old housecoat that is hard to part with. Your baby will be more comfortable with his favorite toy, especially if he goes to a new or "less comfortable" place.

YOU CAN SOMETIMES AVOID BABY'S ATTACHMENT TO A DILAPIDATED TOY BY ONLY PURCHASING WELL-MADE TOYS

There are many toys that adults think are adorable in variety stores. Many of these inexpensive toys are worth only what you pay for them.

IF YOUR SPECIAL BABY LIKES A TOY, HE WILL USE IT FOR YEARS.

SELECT YOUR BABY'S TOYS AS CAREFULLY AS YOU WOULD SELECT YOUR CAR AND YOUR APPLIANCES.

Toys are even more valuable to your baby than the cars and appliances are to you.

YOUR CHILD NEEDS A PLACE OUTSIDE TO PLAY

It is important that your child have a place to **run, climb, and dig in the dirt or sand**.

Swing sets are good play equipment but so are **old tires** (washed so they won't make black marks), **large logs, wagons, trikes, doll buggies, ride-on toys, and wheelbarrows**.

ALLOW YOUR CHILD TO PLAY OUTSIDE AS OFTEN AS POSSIBLE

If it is not raining, too cold, or too hot, your child should play outside every day. Warm, water repellent clothing can keep him warm and dry in cold weather. Sunscreen can protect your baby in hot weather. Make sure that your baby's play clothes allow for freedom of movement—but afford some protection to knees and elbows

It is important that the area be close to the house so you can watch the baby play.

In the beginning you may need to go outside with the baby to be sure that he stays in the play area.

ENJOY PLAY TIME—THE FRESH AIR IS GOOD FOR YOU, TOO

Just before lunch-time or just before nap-
time is a good time for brisk outdoor
play.

If the weather is cool, the middle of the day is
best. If the weather is hot, early or late in
the day is best.

SOME PARENTS FIND THAT A FENCED PLAY YARD GIVES THEM MORE PEACE OF MIND

Remember that children are usually able to figure out how to climb a fence and open a gate.

You may also forget to close the gate. So never trust the play area just because there is a fence.

GOING TO A PARK TO PLAY WOULD BE AN EXCELLENT IDEA. YOUR CHILD CAN LEARN BY WATCHING OTHER CHILDREN PLAY, AND PLAYING WITH THEM

*You may have to be brave to go to the park . . . children and parents may make com-
ments about your baby and what your baby can or can't do. (See "Don't Leave
Home Without It,"* The Exceptional Parent, *June 1978 (page 149).*

Babies learn how one object relates to another

He learns that an object makes a certain
noise and he will look for that object in
the direction of the noise

The baby learns that the blocks have one
color on one side and another color on
the other side.

He learns to find the color of the block that he
likes by turning it to see the other side.

The baby learns that one block will stay on
top of another.

By watching what happens when a toy is dropped he learns that if an object (toy) is released in
a certain way, it will fall to another object (floor) in about the same place *again* and
again.

He will look on the floor to see the toy.

Your role as a parent is to retrieve the toy so he can drop it again. **Obviously the role is
frustrating!**

If you watch your baby closely, you will be able to discover if the goal of his game is to watch
the toy fall or if the goal is to watch mother and father pick up the toy.

THE BABY LEARNS NOT ONLY HOW TO OPERATE THE TOY OBJECTS, BUT HE ALSO LEARNS HOW TO OPERATE YOU!

Learning to do each of these skills is important.

Part of the goal of social interaction is for the baby to learn how to express **what is needed well enough to get others to help supply his needs.**

Some of the baby's needs are food, clothing, and daily care,

BUT SOME OF HIS NEEDS ARE TO SHARE ACTIVITIES AND TO "TALK" TO PEOPLE

IT IS IMPORTANT THAT YOUR BABY LEARN TO COMMUNICATE THESE NEEDS TO YOU AND LATER TO OTHERS

He can learn to do this only if he begins to practice early.

You don't want the baby to learn to control you entirely.

*If you are sure that he has learned to look at the floor to see the object has dropped, and he is now perfecting the skill of controlling you, allow a few turns of the game then terminate by smiling and hugging your baby, looking at the object on the floor, **and** leaving it where the baby dropped it.*

Babies learn to use two objects together.

THE BABY LEARNS THAT ONE OBJECT CAN BE USED TO MAKE ANOTHER OBJECT DO SOMETHING.

He may, for example, learn that it is easier to make a ball move if he hits it with a teddy bear.

It is the beginning of learning that

**spoons and plates are for eating;
soap is for washing;
buttons and button holes are for dressing.**

And that for some social activities

dolls are for hugging;
cups are for drinking;
hats go on the head.

PRACTICING USING TOY OBJECTS IS THE MOST EFFICIENT WAY TO LEARN TO USE THE OBJECTS OF DAILY LIFE

PLAYING TEA PARTY HELPS THE BABY LEARN TO HAVE BETTER EATING SKILLS

DRESSING AND UNDRESSING HELP HIM LEARN HOW TO DRESS

Pulling clothes off and putting on other people's hats and shoes help him learn to dress himself.

Unfortunately undressing is easier and it is learned first.

All babies practice undressing, but special babies need more practice and they frequently undress where other people can see them, even after they are quite big.

You will naturally be embarrassed, but remember that the child is not trying to shock people. He is trying to see how zippers unzip and how buttons unbutton and how pants pull off.

If your baby is still doing this after undressing is learned you may need to plan a way to change his behavior. A teacher or a psychologist can help you make some plans for behavior change (see page 4).

It will probably help if the baby no longer gets attention for undressing. Simply put his clothes back on and say nothing.

Your baby may pick up things in shops or other people's homes and use them as toys

You can't allow your baby to touch and handle things that belong to shops or to other people.

Other people will become frustrated and angry, and your baby will not be learning that some things belong to others and must not be touched.

IT WILL TAKE YOUR CHILD A LONG TIME TO UNDERSTAND THAT SOME THINGS BE-LONG TO OTHER PEOPLE AND MUST NOT BE TOUCHED

Your baby is not trying to annoy you and others—he is just interested in bright, pretty things.

If he picks up or touches something that should not be handled or touched, quietly take the object away or move him out of reach.

If you never take your baby out where he will see pretty and interesting things, he will miss seeing and learning.

So take your baby out to see things but not to the china shop.

Until your child is past the stage of needing to touch in order to learn you will probably want to be careful about where you take him.

You may find it helpful to take some of the baby's favorite toys when you take him out. Then, if the baby has an overwhelming desire to touch something that is untouchable, you can give him one of his favorite toys.

It may be discouraging and you may miss going to some "nonchildren" places. Keep a list of those places and go there when you can have someone else care for the baby.

Although it's true that you and your baby need to see a lot of each other, it's also true that you need a break now and then.

5 SOME BABIES DON'T GET ALONG WELL WITH OTHER BABIES

If your child hits or bites other children, the other children (and their mothers) won't want to be around your baby.

Because, **special babies learn from watching other people**, it is important that your baby have the opportunity to watch other children and the time to learn to communicate with them.

In the book, *The Secret Language of Your Child* by D. Lewis, St. Martin Press, 1978, 1980, there are descriptions of how nursery school children communicate with each other using *body language*. It is important at beginning of learning to first learn to get along with others. If your baby bites or hits other children, it is important that you show him a better way to interact with other children.

If you hit or bite your baby back to show him not to hit or bite, what you are really showing is that **even mommy and daddy bite.**

In order to know what you should do, you must know exactly what was happening at the time that your child hit or bit another child—he may have just been striking back.

SOMETIMES, OTHER CHILDREN TAKE ADVANTAGE OF SPECIAL BABIES BECAUSE THEY ARE NOT ABLE TO DEFEND THEMSELVES. IT MAY BE THAT ANOTHER CHILD WAS TRYING TO DOMINATE YOURS.

HOWEVER, IT IS PROBABLE THAT YOUR CHILD DID NOT KNOW HOW TO EXPRESS HIS NEEDS AND DESIRES TO THE OTHER CHILD.

UNLESS YOU CAN ARRANGE A TIME WHEN YOU CAN CAREFULLY OBSERVE WHAT YOUR CHILD AND OTHER CHILDREN ARE DOING, IT MAY BE HELPFUL TO HAVE A TEACHER OR PSYCHOLOGIST WATCH CLOSELY TO SEE EXACTLY WHAT IS HAPPENING BETWEEN THE CHILDREN TO HELP YOU DECIDE WHAT IS GOING ON.

YOUR SPECIAL CHILD MAY TAKE TOYS AWAY FROM YOUNGER CHILDREN

He may be more interested in the toys of younger children than in the toys of children of his age.

Usually it takes a special baby longer to understand how to use a toy and to learn from using it.

Special children need to play with the same kind of toys that younger children play with.

This may create some confusion in the household if you have younger children.

It will certainly be confusing when you take your baby where there are younger children.

SINCE YOUR CHILD PROBABLY HAS NOT LEARNED THAT THERE MAY BE MORE THAN ONE RED BALL,

he will see any red ball and think it is the same one that he was playing with on the kitchen floor.

Other children may have been using the ball for a game of roly-poly and won't mind having your baby join—but he may not have had enough experiences pushing and following a ball to know that it is possible to push it and have the other person push it back.

You can show him by sitting behind him, pushing the ball and holding the baby to let him wait for the other child to push the ball back—but don't try too long.

Your baby probably needs to explore the use of the ball alone for some time more.

It will help to carefully label all of your baby's toys. You can use a permanent felt-tip marker, a wood burner, or a metal engraver. It is wise to label the toy with the child's initials or name. When there is a toy that your baby especially likes, it is wise to get another just like it for ready substitution when it "wears out."

When your baby will be with other children take his favorite toys.

It is usually an advantage to the special baby to have other children in the family. He can usually learn to get along with other people better if there are brothers and sisters in the family. However many parents of special children worry about the effect they may have on the other children.

Older children—If you already have children they will probably play the role played by most older children—helping to care for the younger child. It will be easy to expect them to learn to help so much with the special baby that they will not have time to do things for themselves. Allow the other children plenty of time *to learn* to do things for themselves. Allow them plenty of time to study, play, and be with their friends. If you have several older children they might take turns helping with the special child just as they would take turns helping to do the dishes.

Having more children—Sometimes parents of a special child wonder whether they should have more children. If the condition is inherited, a discussion with a genetic counselor may be helpful. It will be necessary to plan carefully to be sure that the mother has sufficient health to care for more children and that the family will have enough income for more children. Usually families who have a special baby and then a younger child enjoy the younger child even more than they otherwise might have done.

Helping with the special child—Regardless of whether other children are older or younger, it is always difficult to try to be sure that the special child does not take up too much family time. It is not wise to have family life centered totally around the special needs of the special child. It is difficult to balance the needs of one child against the needs of another. If your special baby hits the other children or takes things from them, treat the situation as normal. Never expect the other children in the family to accept behavior from the special baby that you would not allow from the other children.

Talking about the problems—As the other children get older tell them about the conditions that caused the baby's problems and talk to them about family plans and things that must be adjusted in the house. Listen to their suggestions and hear their frustrations. Growing up has never been easy, and growing up with a special brother or sister is a little like being expected to be grown-up while you are growing up. There is an article by V. Hayden, "The Other Children," in *The Exceptional Parent*, 1974, 4(4) 26-29. A sister tells of her experiences being a "second mother." In the chapter "Working with Siblings in the School" by C. T. Michaelis, *Home and School Partnerships in Exceptional Education*, Rockville, MD, 1980, there is a discussion about how other children feel.

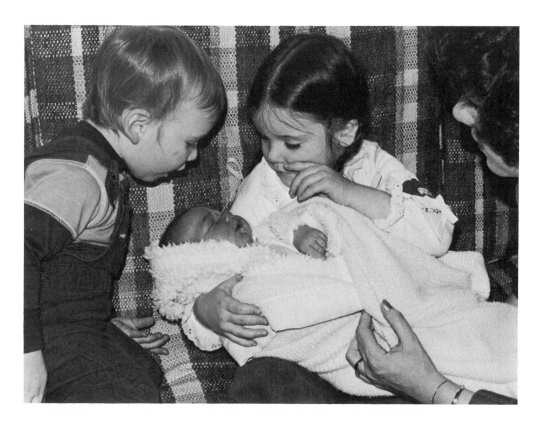

6 SOME SPECIAL BABIES WANT TO CONTROL THEIR PARENTS' TIME

There are some things that babies do to make sure that their parents pay attention to them.

He may fuss or cry all the time

He may fuss when mother goes away or takes care of other children.

He may keep getting into things so mother has to follow him and stop him.

He may keep dropping things so mother has to pick them up

Or he may not eat unless he is fed in a certain way.

It is important to be sure that the baby is safe and doesn't really need anything. But it is not good to run to him every time he fusses.

If you are sure that the baby is all right, let him fuss. Don't feel that you must jump the minute he fusses.

It will not hurt him to cry for awhile or to wait while you finish taking care of another child or finish a household task—or even until you finish reading the paper.

Some special babies hold their breath until they turn blue

A baby who is not breathing is sure to get everyone's attention.

IF YOUR BABY STOPS BREATHING IT IS IMPORTANT TO FIND OUT WHY

Check to see if there is something stuck in the baby's mouth. Have a doctor, nurse, or respiration therapist see if there is some obstruction in the baby's mouth or breathing passages.

It doesn't happen very often but don't rule out the possibility that the baby has learned to hold his breath because

EVERYONE MAKES A FUSS OVER THE BABY WHEN HE IS NOT BREATHING

If your baby has learned to hold his breath watch to see what is happening.

Does he want you to pick him up?

Does he want you to stop feeding cereal?

Does he want to be played with?

Sometimes babies who are **having trouble learning to tell other people what they want** don't know other ways to make people look at them and see what they want.

> **Help your baby tell you by watching him** and offering the care that you think he needs and telling him the words for the care— get a drink—go outside.

>> This will help your baby learn to tell you or show you want he wants.

> **When you are sure that the baby is getting what he needs**; and you are trying to understand when he tries to show you what he needs; then you don't have to be upset if he wants even more attention.

You should not feel guilty for not spending all your time with your baby—you need to do other things,

and the baby needs to learn that it is not possible to always control someone.

Of course you don't want your baby to feel neglected.

It is helpful to have a place for the child to play close to where you will be working or reading (see page 113).

You can expect him to play with a toy or listen to music at times when you need to be doing other things.

If your baby holds his breath for no physical cause, you can usually get him breathing again by picking him up and shaking him firmly but gently.

If he has held his breath for a long time, you may need to do **CPR** (see page 14). Sometimes children can control holding breath and can resume breathing at will.

It is important that you behave matter-of factly when a child holds his breath.

> Whether the baby seems to be holding his breath on purpose or not, it is not a good idea for him to be able to feel stress or concern from you.

> Treat the situation as calmly as possible. Attend to the child then go on about your routine.

This will not be easy.

> *The natural response of a parent to a baby who is not breathing is upset and concern.*

> *If you are upset and concerned you will not be able to tell whether your baby needs help or not and you will be teaching him that it is possible to get a lot of attention by simply taking a deep breath and holding it.*

Elementary school children sometimes play the breath holding game. When they stop breathing for a long enough period, they pass out. As soon as they pass out, however, breathing resumes automatically. It is not healthy because the body needs oxygen from breathing all the time.

The best way to stop the breath holding game is to pay little attention to it and to encourage others to ignore it.

Some special babies will sleep only in their parents' bed. All babies like to sleep in bed with their parents.

Years ago many babies did sleep with parents on cold nights, but when they got older, they usually tired of the parents' bed and were happier in a bed of their own.

Sometimes special babies enjoy sleeping in the parents' bed so much that they will sleep only when they are in their parents' bed.

Sometimes parents worry about the baby at night and think that it is "safer" to have him in their bed (see Sleep Problems, page 45).

IT IS USUALLY WISER FOR THE BABY TO SLEEP ALONE

Most babies fuss about going to bed from time to time.

It will not hurt your special baby to cry a little when he is put to bed.

Make sure he is comfortable and has what he needs, then let the baby fuss.

Even when babies are very young they can learn to do things to get attention.

Be sure that you give your child all the care and love that he needs—then ignore his cries to let him sleep in your bed.

It is important that parents have some time alone together to enjoy each other and to talk about things other than the baby.

When you are calm and comfortable about your childs' sleeping in his own bed, the baby will be, too.

VI

Most Special Babies
Have Trouble
Learning To Talk

1 MOST SPECIAL BABIES HAVE TROUBLE LEARNING TO TALK

Children with hearing problems probably will have problems with all types of language and speech (see page 182).

SOME SPECIAL BABIES DON'T SEEM TO UNDERSTAND WHAT PEOPLE ARE SAYING SOMETIMES THEY DON'T SEEM TO KNOW WHEN YOU ARE TALKING.

Be sure that you are close enough to your baby so he can see your face

because babies eyes must learn to focus to see clearly.

Young babies and children with special problems frequently cannot see as far as we think they can.

Newborns can only focus and "see" things that are about 6 inches from their faces.

Things farther away appear as a blur to the baby.

When babies are first learning to understand what people say,

They must be able to see faces to help them know if what is said is happy, sad, angry, or if the speaker is tired.

Be sure that other noises will not make it hard
for your baby to hear you.

If the radio, television, or stereo is loud, the child will have trouble differentiating the sound of your voice from all the other sounds.

If you like to listen to music, or the radio, or have television on, keep them as far from the baby's play area as possible and

KEEP IT TURNED DOWN LOW

Then, when you talk to the baby, move close to him and talk to him as if it were a private, special message.

You *can* talk to your baby even when you are not close to him.

He needs to hear your voice from a distance, too. To really learn to understand what you say, however, baby needs to hear your voice up close so he can hear the differences in the sounds of the words.

Babies learn to understand very slowly what people are saying!

Your baby's favorite word will probably be his **name,**

because he will hear it over and over again,

and each time he hears his name someone will be looking at him and smiling.

The more you look, smile, and talk to your
baby and say his name, the sooner he
will respond with pleasure to his name.
And the sooner he will learn to answer
by smiling, or cooing or reaching out his
arms to be picked up.

If your baby does not smile, coo, or reach out when you say his name,

and if he doesn't seem to be aware that you have said his name,

it is natural that you will feel unhappy and discouraged.

*But remember that your baby will learn to understand better when you are happy and
enthusiastic. If you are, what you say will be more interesting to the baby.*

**Be sure to touch your baby when you are talking to him. If seeing and hearing are part of your
childs' problems, he will learn from touching.** Even if your child learns to see and hear as
other babies do, touching helps him to know when you are going to say something to
him.

Encourage others to hold your child and talk to him using his name.

Since your baby will be learning to understand tone of voice as well as the sound of voice,
it is important that he hear high voices, low voices, loud, and soft voices repeat his name
while someone smiles and touches him.

That way he will learn that there is something special about the sound of his name

NO MATTER WHO SAYS IT

YOUR BABY MAY NOT DO WHAT YOU TELL HIM TO

Some special babies have trouble understanding what you want.

Your friends may be able to tell their child
things like:

hand me the ball open your mouth
sit down now let me see.

and the baby will do what the parent asks.

Your child may not be able to understand
what the words mean.

He may see it as a game and run away or
laugh or just stare at you.

He may not even look at you.

You will probably be embarrassed when someone sees you ask the baby to do something and he seems to ignore you. He probably is not really ignoring you. He may not be able to understand your words or he may be satisfied by the mere fact that you are watching him and he may enjoy being watched.

It is possible that he may not know that you are watching. Try not to care about the opinion of others.

When you want to let your baby know that you are busy with something but you find that he still wants your undivided attention despite your repeated efforts to explain that you are busy, **you will feel angry.** *It won't help to punish him. If you punish him, he will be less likely to want to learn what you need to teach him.*

HELP YOUR BABY KNOW WHAT YOU WANT BY SHOWING HIM

When you want the baby to hand you a ball,
hold his arm, say, "(Name), hand me the
ball" and **move his arm to help him
hand you the ball.**

Hold him gently and firmly by the shoulders
and **help him sit down** while you say,
"(Name), sit down,"

Remember—use the baby's name, then
smile and tell him, **"THANK YOU".**

It will take many many attempts, but if you keep repeating and showing him, the baby will gradually learn what you mean.

He will not be able to *do* **what you want until he** *knows* **what you want.**

YOUR BABY MAY NOT MAKE SOUNDS OR TRY TO TALK LIKE OTHER BABIES

It is still important that you talk to him.

Babies learn to understand things before they learn to say them.

Before your child can say, "More drink" he will have to know what *you mean* when *you ask,* "More drink?" He will have to be able to answer you by opening his mouth, reaching out his hand, or pulling away when you ask, "More drink?"

Part of the reason that your baby understands is that you are holding a bottle or glass so the baby can drink.

To help your baby learn to repeat your words, you must clearly say the words to him while you do what the words mean. You must show the baby at the same time that you tell him.

When you say, "**No, no**" you expect your baby to stop whatever he is doing but

Your special baby may have trouble knowing what "no, no" means. When you say "No," he may behave as he does when you say his name.

Some babies have trouble learning to respond in one way to one word and in a different way to another word—**this makes it more difficult to take care of the child.**

it also makes talking to your baby less enjoyable but that doesn't mean you should stop talking!

If you do, the child will not have a chance to learn that one set of sounds means one thing and another set of sounds means an other thing.

It will help him learn if you

HUG OR PAT YOUR BABY WHEN YOU SAY HIS NAME AND FROWN AND SHAKE YOUR HEAD WHEN YOU SAY, "NO, NO".

Try not to be too discouraged if your baby does not seem to be learning—just keep trying and trying.

It is very difficult for some babies to learn what "No" and "Not" and "Never" mean.

Your baby will learn faster if you show him what you mean by doing the action at the same time that you are saying the words.

Put on an exaggerated frown put your hands on your hips, lean forward, and hold a steady, firm gaze.

Don't confuse the baby by laughing and cuddling at this time.

IT WILL ALSO HELP TO SAY, "NO, NO" ONLY WHEN THE BABY IS IN DANGER AND THERE IS A REAL "EMERGENCY."

Arrange safe play areas (see pages 111-114), put away objects that may be dangerous, and have safe toys for your baby.

Then you will only need to say, "No, no" for real emergencies.

It is almost as if the baby doesn't know that words have meaning.

He may not be able to tell the difference between sounds that people make when they speak and other sounds that are happening all the time.

If your baby does not differentiate the sounds of words from the sounds of the dishwasher, the fan, or the doorbell, then he will not:

Look at you when you talk to him	**Coo back when you hum or sing to him**
Smile when you talk to him	**Stop when you say, "No, no"**

If your baby does not listen, dance, sway, or
clap to music, he may be having trouble
hearing sounds of all kinds.

**Have a trained audiologist with special equip-
ment test your baby's hearing.**

If he does not hear well, it is important that
you have someone show you how you
can talk to the baby and play with him to
help him learn in the most effective
ways.

It is also possible that your baby does not look at you, or smile or coo or stop when you say,
"No, no" because he has not learned what the sounds mean.

He will need more talking and smiling and talking and doing until he finally understands what
words and actions mean.

*You will be discouraged and think that your child doesn't enjoy being with you like other
babies enjoy being with their parents.*

*The problem really is, however, that your baby does not know **how** to express feelings.*

*Continue to express your feelings, so your child will have an example to follow. Try to
realize that he does love you, even though he does not have a way to show you.*

Your baby may not wave bye-bye as other babies do.

One of the first things people expect infants to learn to do is to wave bye-bye. Most babies learn
to do this when they are only a few months old.

Your child may have trouble doing this, or he
may wave only when someone is willing
to stand and wait a long time.

Some babies may wave bye-bye to everyone
whether it is time to wave or not.

*When that happens people may look
strangely at you and the baby.*

*Try to ignore their stares. There are
many people who are bothered by **all**
children.*

Keep waving bye-bye to your baby when it is appropriate. This will help the baby learn that
certain ideas and activities can be represented by some action.

Going can be represented by waving.
No can be represented by shaking the head.
Yes can be represented by nodding the head.
I like you can be represented by blowing a kiss.

For some special babies learning to use the hands to represent ideas and activities may be the most effective way in which they can communicate with others.

Some special babies have trouble

>**Saying nursery rhymes,
>singing,
>and doing finger play.**

It is fun for the parent and child to do these things but **if your baby doesn't want to, you may feel that he doesn't enjoy being with you.**

THE PROBLEM REALLY MAY BE THAT HE IS NOT ABLE TO SIT STILL LONG ENOUGH

Try having books handy to show the baby for very brief times—perhaps while you both are sitting on the floor or riding in the car.

Special children usually take longer to be interested in nursery rhymes, singing, and doing finger play.

Don't stop trying; just make the sessions very brief.

You can recite nursery rhymes and sing to the baby while you are working around the house or while you are feeding him.

Some special children will not sit still while you play "This Little Piggie" with their fingers and toes.

It may be that your child is very sensitive to touch and needs to become accustomed to being touched. Try using some desensitization ideas on page 25.

Try not to be discouraged—your baby is not purposely slow. He may want to do them even more than you do but **it is very hard for him**.

Your baby may not be able to play "Show Me Your Nose."

He may merely point to his face or put his hands in the air or stare at you.

He may do this even when he is much older than your friends' babies who have been able to play "Show Me Your Nose" for a long time.

It is natural for you to feel disappointed and not to want other people to see your baby making mistakes and looking silly.

It is important, however, to show your child
how to find the different parts of his
body.

He will learn only if you keep asking and
showing.

ONE OF THE BEST WAYS TO TALK ABOUT FINGERS, HANDS, EYES, AND NOSE AND INDICATE THEM

is while you are wiping his nose and
washing his hands and face.

The album "Adaptive Behavior—Self Help"
from Kimbo Educational has a song
about wiping the nose and another
about washing the hands and face and
taking a bath.

Singing songs and playing that you are washing and wiping is good practice.

If your baby is not able to move his arms and hands to touch his nose, help him to move them with your hands while you sing songs together.

2 BABIES LEARN TO MAKE SOUNDS WHEN THEY SEE AND HEAR OTHERS MAKE SOUNDS

They learn to organize coos and hums to sound like the noises they hear.

Some special children don't making cooing and gooing sounds.

It is important to help your baby learn to coo and goo.

A child begins to learn to control sounds when he observes that adults repeat the sound that the baby makes.

That way he learns to organize the coos and goos so they eventually become the sounds of words.

You can help your child do this by repeating back to him the coo, hum, or squeal that he makes.

The baby will begin to notice when you are

MAKING HIS SOUND

and he will respond, subsequently every-time you talk to the baby,

HE WILL ANSWER WITH HIS SOUND

Gradually your child will begin to answer you with sounds that approximate the sounds you are making and he will begin to organize these sounds into mama and bye-bye and even mm-oore.

If you and your baby play the sound game back and forth, his sounds will gradually become more and more like yours. This takes a long time for all babies.

But for special babies, it takes even longer to be able to imitate the sounds the parents make.

3 IT MAY NOT BE POSSIBLE FOR SOME SPECIAL BABIES TO LEARN TO MAKE SOUNDS AND SAY WORDS AS OTHER BABIES DO.

They may understand more than they are able to say.

There are many sounds they may never be able to produce because of damage to mouth, teeth, vocal cords, or brain control of the vocal structure.

You will feel depressed that your baby cannot say things that other babies say and you will probably need to talk about it to a friend—and to cry about it.

However, you should not show how you feel to your baby. You must act as if it is natural to not be able to make sounds.

If you keep talking to your child, he will learn
to be able to understand much of what
you say.

**Your baby may be able to communicate
through actions.**

He may be able to learn to put things away
when you tell him to do so.

He may learn to shake his head "no,"
even if he is not able to say "No."

Even if your baby is not able to move enough to put things away or shake his head, he can learn to tell you things by the way he looks at you.

In this way he is talking to you—not with words, but through actions. Be sure that you listen by watching and answering the baby.

YOUR BABY MAY NOT REPEAT WHAT YOU SAY

When babies are small they usually repeat what they hear other people say.

Your special child may not do this.

When you look at your baby, talk to him, show him the teddy bear, and tell him to say "teddy," the baby may look blankly at you.

It is natural for you to feel hurt but try not to let your child feel that you are unhappy with him or that you do not like him.

Try to be brave, continue to smile and talk to your baby.

Some babies need to hear a word many many times before they want to play with the sound of the word.

When you are playing with your child, repeat the names of a few things that are interesting to him.

The baby is more likely to learn to say **the name of a favorite toy** than the name of a least favored vegetable.

If you tell him the names of too many things at the same time, he will be confused. **Choose some of the baby's favorite things and keep repeating their names**.

The more interesting you make words sound, the more likely the baby will say the sound.

IT MAY BE HARD TO UNDERSTAND YOUR BABY.

Many times when special babies try to talk they make sounds and move their faces but the sounds aren't words.

This can be very upsetting.

You want to understand the baby and you know that he wants to tell you something, but you can't understand what it is.

Try not to show your child how unhappy and frustrated that makes you feel. Try to smile and be pleasant. Look around, think about what has been happening, and try to guess what the baby is trying to tell you. Then answer him as naturally as you can.

As your child gets older you may ask him to "tell me again."

However, if the repetition is no easier to understand, you should guess and respond to the baby.

Don't keep asking him to repeat.

That can be such an unpleasant experience that the next time he wants to tell you something, he may hesitate in anticipation of demands for repetition.

If the baby doesn't begin to be easier to understand in a few months you may want to have a speech therapist and an oral surgeon examine your baby's mouth to see if it is formed in such a way that it is especially difficult for him to talk.

Sometimes surgery can help but it is common for most special babies to have difficulty making the tongue, mouth, and vocal cords work well together.

YOUR BABY MAY POINT AT THINGS.

When babies are learning that different objects have different names, they can become frustrated because they do not know the right name for the object, so they point.

All babies point when they are learning.

Because special babies take longer to learn words, they may need to point for a longer time.

It is often difficult to know at what the child is pointing. There may be many things in the general direction.

Try to be patient and figure out what the child wants to indicate.

Sometimes it helps to take the baby close to the objects so he can touch the specific object. Or you might touch what you think the baby might mean.

Often this can be frustrating because when you take the baby up close, he may no longer be interested.

As you take the baby up close or as you go close:
   touch the object,
   say the name of the object.

Be patient and plan to do it again and again—today and tomorrow and the next day.

This may embarrass you around other people especially in public or when visiting someone whom you do not know well. It is natural to feel that way and there may be sometimes when you would not want to get up and move around (e.g. church service). In most public places, however, and at the home of relatives and close friends it should be acceptable. It will be understood that you need to teach your baby.

Remember all those other people are not very important to your baby.

Of course you wish that your baby could speak clearly enough for others to understand— maybe later he will be able to do that.

Now, however, it is important that he knows you understand and it is important that you accept his utterances as if they were normal and ordinary—just as if he were saying the "right" words.

If you "listen" to your baby, it will help him learn to listen to you and want to do the things you ask.

If your baby only makes sounds or gestures for things, don't be discouraged.

He may fold his arms and rock them back and forth to indicate his favorite teddy bear.

He may try to tell you what he wants by sitting on the floor near the refrigerator.

He may pull his coat from the closet to show that he wants to go out.

Making sounds—even if they are not the
"real" sounds for an object or activity is
the beginning of learning to make the
"real sounds."

Many babies call the car "bye-bye" or the blanket "blankey."

They usually have certain sounds or syllables to call members of the family.

These actions and sounds are the beginning of learning adult actions and sounds.

Respect the baby's desire to tell you something! Do not respond by correcting the baby, but
do what would be appropriate and say the appropriate words as if the baby's message
was clear.

4 YOUR BABY MAY NOT SMILE AND COO TO STRANGERS

Many people like babies and smile and talk to them in stores or on busses or in restaurants.

MANY SPECIAL BABIES DON'T SMILE AND COO BACK

Sometimes they merely stare at the other person.
Sometimes they turn their heads away.
Sometimes they cry.

All babies do those things sometimes, but if yours does these things all the time,
you will feel like crying, too.

You may feel that you are not a good parent—and that your baby is strange and different.

> *Try to remember that most people who talk to children have had many children not answer.*

> *Most of them have had experience with children for many years and it is quite likely that they have talked to special babies before.*

Some people may talk to your child because they know that he is special.

They want to encourage you by paying attention to your baby.

Even if you are embarrassed
try not to be so uncomfortable that you do not take your baby out where other people are.

He needs to have new experiences in order to learn. The article "Don't Leave Home Without It" by Carol Michaelis in the *Exceptional Parent*, June, 1978 tells some of the things that your baby can learn by going out. It also tells about how parents of special babies feel when they take their babies out.

VII

Some Babies Are Very Difficult To Care For

1 IT IS DIFFICULT TO BATHE AND WASH SOME BABIES

Most babies squirm and splash in the bath water and it is important to take care that they don't slip into the water.

Bathing takes the full attention of whoever is bathing the baby.

SPECIAL BABIES ARE EVEN MORE DIFFICULT TO BATHE

They may go stiff and rigid and be hard to hold.

> You may need to adapt the way you hold him in the bathtub. (See page 73 for suggestions.)

> Your special baby may be limp and keep slipping into the bath water.

> The lying down shower explained on page 74 may be a good way to bathe the limp child.

Some special babies eat soap bars as if they were candy bars.

> You may need to put liquid soap in the bath water and keep soap bars out of sight.

> **Some special babies like to put their faces into the water.** They may not pull them out—even to breathe.

> Some even put their faces into the water and inhale. This, of course, is dangerous.

Many children have drowned by slipping into their own bath water. It is easier for a special baby to slip.

You will need to be very careful setting up the bath and arranging time so you can give it your full attention. (See suggestions, pages 73-74.)

Never leave your baby alone in the bath water—even for a few seconds.

NEVER PUT HIM INTO THE BATH WATER BEFORE MAKING SURE THAT IT IS NOT TOO HOT

Many special babies have sensitive skin and should not bathe in water as hot as you might.

Special babies may have trouble either knowing or telling you that the water is too hot.

If you are not sure about being able to determine how hot the water should be, test it with a thermometer.

Do not allow your child to play with the faucet while you are bathing him.

Many babies have been accidentally burned because they ran hot water into the tub.

BATH TIME MIGHT BE A GOOD TIME TO GET DAD INVOLVED

Sometimes you might need an extra set of hands. Other times it might be a respite for mother.

Before you start the process, put on clothing that will not be spoiled by getting wet. You may want to wear a rubber or plastic apron. (Try it first. It could be slippery and make holding the baby difficult. In warm or humid weather it could be too warm.)

It will help to have a bath area that can take some splashes and plenty of clean towels!

THEN—TRY TO ENJOY IT!

Playing in the bath water is a good learning experience for any baby, but for a baby with motor problems it is not only play time, it is

THERAPY TIME

because he can move more freely in warm water than he can move out of the water.

Babies who have trouble seeing, can develop their sense of touch with a wet rubber duckie, wet washcloth, sponge, and plastic boat with a small sail.

It is a good time to practice pouring with plastic measuring cups,

and pushing a rubber ball that floats on top of the water.

Babies who have trouble hearing may have more trouble in the bath because noises made by the water may mask what you say to them.

Because of all the extra difficulty

IT IS EASY TO SEE BATHING AS A NUISANCE

and want to **skip it now and then.**

Try to **keep the bath as a daily activity.** Bathing is especially important to special children because they often do not complain about itching or other discomfort.

Their skin can develop rashes and open sores very easily, also.

Wash your baby carefully making sure that you get into all the folds of the skin.

It is very important that his skin be dried very carefully and thoroughly to keep it healthy.

SPECIAL BABIES SOMETIMES NEED MORE THAN ONE BATH A DAY

They spill food on themselves, have more toilet accidents, and drool on their clothes causing them to smell bad.

If you want to keep your baby clean, it will be necessary to bathe him more than once on some days.

Sometimes it may seem as though you just get the bath cleaned up when the baby needs another one.

Try to take it calmly—he is not causing the extra work on purpose.

It is natural for bath time to seem like a chore now and then, but try not to see it as a chore every time.

Try to see it as a time to keep the baby clean—but also as a time to talk and play with him. It is one of the best times for him to learn about parts of the body. There is a song about taking a bath on the Kimbo Educational Record, "Adaptive Behavior—Self Help."

Arrange for someone else to take care of the baby's bath now and then and you do something that you enjoy—just for yourself

You can then come back and face the daily bath with renewed enthusiasm.

2 IT IS DIFFICULT TO TOILET TRAIN SOME CHILDREN AND YOUR SPECIAL BABY IS LIKELY TO BE ONE OF THEM

You will probably want to keep your child in diapers longer than most.

Although it is wise to wait until you and your baby are ready, it is important to help him learn good toilet habits.

As he grows older the ability to take care of toileting needs may be one of the most *valuable* skills that he can have.

YOUR SPECIAL BABY MAY NOT WANT TO SIT ON THE TOILET OR HE MAY LIKE SITTING ON THE TOILET, BUT HE MAY NOT DO ANYTHING

He may then have an "accident" in his pants as soon as he gets off the toilet.

Or your baby may soil his pants, then play in it. All babies do this from time to time, but yours might do it most of the time.

TOILET TRAINING IS NOT SOMETHING THAT CAN BE DONE SOME TIMES

In order to be effective, toilet training must be done

ALL THE TIME

If you are not ready to deal with the baby's toilet habits all day, every day, it is better to wait and keep him in diapers for awhile longer.

Exactly how long you keep your baby in diapers is up to you.

It will depend on your baby's health and your health.

It will depend on how convenient the bathroom is.

It will depend on whether your child is in a school program and the school is ready to help you teach your child to use the toilet.

If you are expecting a new baby right away, if you must have surgery, or if you are planning a vacation, it is probably wise to wait until the "unusual" event is over.

But take care that you don't have one "unusual" event after another.

No one really **enjoys** toilet training. It takes time and patience **even for those children who are easy to train**.

TOILET TRAINING IS NO PICNIC—EVEN WHEN IT GOES WELL

Your baby will be ready to begin toilet training as soon as his diaper is dry for at least two hours at a time. Then the bladder is large enough to hold some urine and the muscles are developed enough to open and close the opening to the bladder. Usually by this time the baby also has regular bowel movements once or twice a day and he usually urinates at the same time that he has a bowel movement.

YOU CAN HELP YOUR BABY DEVELOP REGULAR ELIMINATION BY

Feeding him at the same time very day,
Giving him extra liquids to drink at the same time every day,
Putting him to sleep at the same time every day, and
Seeing that he has plenty of opportunity to move and play.

In order to eliminate regularly your baby needs plenty of fresh fruits and vegetables and some cereal to create bulk.

If your baby has difficulty moving his bowels regularly, your doctor may be able to help with a special diet.

If you have tried to help your child develop regular elimination habits but he doesn't seem to be responding,

ask your doctor to examine the baby to see if there are some special problems

that would make elimination more difficult.

Some children who have physical problems may not be able to control the muscles of elimination and they may need to accomplish elimination in other ways (see Spina Bifida, page 192).

However, most babies—even special babies—can learn to use the toilet to eliminate.

Even babies who cannot talk well enough to tell you they need to go can tell you in other ways.

Even those who cannot move well enough to get to the toilet can let you know when they want you to take them or can learn to go when you put them on regularly.

Even babies who cannot sit well enough to sit up on the toilet can learn to use the toilet if some support is developed to hold them in place (see Cerebral palsy, page 172).

You will need to have a potty chair for the child.

Many parents find that a molded plastic chair that sits on the floor is good because it balances well and it is possible to clean it thoroughly.

Most children will be more successful learn-ing in a chair that sits on the floor rather than a small seat that sits on the adult toilet.

If your child can put his feet on the floor, he will be more secure.

If your child is not able to sit up without help,
   you will need to have some extra support for him.

> You may even need to have a potty chair built that has higher sides and has a seat belt attached to the seat (see Cerebral palsy, page 172).

If the child does not feel secure and comfortable, he cannot use the potty.

If your home has more than one level or if you are active in various parts of the house, it may be helpful to have identical potty chairs located in several convenient places.

Some parents find it helpful to put potty chairs in rooms other than bathrooms.

> Although this may be helpful in the learning process, it may be difficult later because the child will learn to think that it is acceptable to eliminate in places other than bathrooms.

IT MAY BE DIFFICULT TO RETEACH THE BABY LATER TO ELIMINATE IN THE BATHROOM ONLY

Because you will need to remove them more frequently and you will want your baby to learn to take his pants down, to use the potty.

YOUR BABY WILL NEED TO HAVE SOME CLOTHING THAT IS EASY TO REMOVE

Two-piece clothing is the most efficient.

You and the baby can slide pants down and pull them up without totally undressing the child.

Pants that have elastic at the top
   are quicker to use because it is not necessary to open and close fasteners.

When you decide to begin toilet training it is

TIME TO PUT YOUR CHILD IN TRAINING PANTS

it is wise to find some that are made of **thick terry cloth**, so accidents won't be too messy.

If your child is older and larger than most children who are being potty trained, you may need to make some training pants out of terry toweling.

Be sure that all the child's clothes are washable.

You will likely need more changes of pants than changes of shirts.

You will need extra socks and it may help to have a pair of shoes to wear when one is drying, because sometimes accidents soil shoes and socks as well as pants.

YOUR BABY MAY HAVE TROUBLE LEARNING HOW A FULL BLADDER FEELS AND WHEN HIS BOWELS ARE READY TO MOVE

You may have to help him learn to recognize these feelings.

If you put your baby on the potty at regular, frequent intervals, he will probably urinate or have a bowel movement while on the potty.

You can then hug and praise the baby, telling him, "Good! Pee-pee in the potty" or whatever words you feel comfortable using. It usually helps to use one word to describe urination and another for bowel movements

If you are uncomfortable with the words commonly used to describe elimination, you may want to make up a new word.

If you do this you will not only need to teach the word to your baby but to others who might come in contact with him so they can talk to your baby, too.

It will be easier for him if you use a word that other people use and

if you use the same word over and over again.

When you decide to begin potty training

DON'T STOP

unless you have a family emergency or unless your child gets seriously ill.

Make it a routine.

PUT YOUR CHILD ON THE POTTY EVERY HOUR FOR NO MORE THAN FIVE MINUTES AT A TIME

Put him on the potty first thing in the morning
before meals
after meals

at mid-morning
at mid-afternoon

at bathtime
and before bedtime

Although you may find the routine time-consuming, **don't let your child know it.** Try to make the experience pleasant for both of you.

LEAD RATHER THAN CARRY YOUR CHILD TO THE BATHROOM

If the child walks on his own, it helps him feel
that he is doing it "all by myself."

Say, "Johnny—bathroom."
When the child is in front of the potty,
guide his hands in pulling down his
pants so he will begin to see how to **do it
alone.**

Say, "Down come Johnny's pants."

Put your child on the potty or help him onto
the potty.

Stay in the bathroom with your child, but do
not talk to him or distract him with toys.

Since you will be waiting in the bathroom
many times during the day, you might
want to keep a favorite book or maga-
zine close by so you can occupy yourself.

**At first you may want a clock or timer in the
bathroom** to be sure you leave the child
on the potty long enough.

Take care not to leave him so long that he
gets bored and begins to play with toilet
paper—or whatever else is handy.

Remember, if the child sits on the potty
**longer than five minutes, he will have
difficulty learning what the potty chair
is for.**

AFTER THE CHILD HAS BEEN SITTING ON THE POTTY FOR FIVE MINUTES

Wipe his bottom and remove him from the potty.

Say, **"Now Johnny gets up."** Guide the child's hands to help you pull up his pants and say,
"Pull up Johnny's pants." Empty the potty and rinse it out.

Your child may want to assist you by holding onto the potty while you are emptying it.

If he wants to help, let him. He will learn to feel responsible for the whole bathroom procedure.

Help him wash his hands. Say, **"Clean hands, Johnny."**

If your child doesn't want to stay long enough to help you empty and wash out the potty, wash
his hands immediately after taking him off the potty, then clean the potty.

BE SURE THAT YOU WASH YOUR HANDS BEFORE YOU START TO DO OTHER THINGS IN THE HOUSEHOLD

Most special babies have greater difficulty fighting germs than other babies. If you don't wash carefully with soap after toileting, you may spread germs.

YOU MAY WANT TO USE THE REGULAR TOILET FOR TOILET TRAINING

If your child is large enough to sit comfortably on the toilet and can sit without support, it would probably be wise to use it alone for training.

You may want to use the regular toilet with a smaller seat attached to it.

A small stool could be kept in front of the toilet and the child could use it as a step stool and a foot rest while sitting on the toilet. It will be more comfortable for your child if he has a place to rest his feet.

Boys can sometimes handle toileting better by sitting backwards on the seat, facing the back of the toilet.

After five minutes wipe your child and help him get off the toilet.

NEVER FLUSH THE TOILET WHILE THE CHILD IS SITTING ON IT

AFTER EACH POTTY EXPERIENCE, HUG YOUR CHILD—WHETHER THE EXPERIENCE WAS SUCCESSFUL OR NOT

YOUR CHILD WILL HAVE ACCIDENTS—

All children do; but yours will probably have more accidents than other children.

It might be a good idea to use *Scotch Guard* on your furniture and carpet before you start to potty train your child. It would also be wise to put off buying new carpet for a while.

Be prepared for accidents by always having several sets of training pants and outer clothes clean and ready to wear.

If you have an automatic washer and dryer in the house, it is much more practical to wash frequently than it is to buy enough clothes for several days.

When your child has an accident, do not scold him. Clean up the mess as quickly and quietly as you can.

THE TIME TO RESPOND TO YOUR CHILD IS WHEN HE IS SUCCESSFUL IN THE BATHROOM

He will want to repeat whatever gets your attention. If you seem to be more interested in the messes than the successes, he will continue to make messes in order to get your attention.

BEFORE LONG, YOU WILL FEEL THAT YOU HAVE BEEN LIVING IN THE BATHROOM

But **don't** give up and **don't** let the baby take a **holiday from training.**

> **From time-to-time have someone else take over.** If the routine is fixed, it will be easy to have someone else take over and give you a chance to be somewhere other than the bathroom.

> > Be sure, however, that your child goes to the bathroom **every hour—all day, every day**, even **Sundays** and **holidays**.

BECAUSE YOUR SPECIAL CHILD MAY BE DEPENDENT IN SOME WAYS FOR MANY YEARS

it will be worth the effort to help him learn good toilet habits when he is young.

There are some songs in the record album, *Adaptive Behavior—Self Help* by C. T. Michaelis, KIM 8055, Long Branch New Jersey, Kimbo Educational 1979, about using the bathroom and washing hands that may help make toileting less tedious.

If your child is in a school program, it will be necessary for the teachers and aides to follow your toilet training routine—the same routine that you use at home.

Write out exactly how you want your child's toilet training to be done at school

Make several copies and take them to the

INDIVIDUALIZED EDUCATIONAL PLAN (IEP) PLANNING MEETING

Ask that the toileting program be part of your child's educational plan.

> **You should not sign the IEP** unless you are satisfied with the plans.

> > You can withhold your signature, and therefore your approval of the plan, if the school is not willing to provide toilet training as you would like to have it done.

A school cannot refuse to take your child because his toilet habits are not acceptable to the school. The school is required to take *all children* and give them the training that their evaluations show as appropriate and that their parents think the child needs.

It may be helpful to you and the school if you offer to help get enough potty chairs or more lavatories for the special students. If the school cannot help your child learn good toilet skills, it probably cannot help him progress to other basic skills.

3 IT MAY BE DIFFICULT TO DRESS YOUR BABY

Babies move much more easily when they don't have clothes on. They can twist, turn, and climb better without clothes.

Most babies prefer not wearing clothes.

It is often a struggle to hold your child long enough to dress him.

SPECIAL BABIES ARE EVEN HARDER TO DRESS

Your special baby might go stiff and push his head and shoulders back when you try to dress him.

> His arms and legs might go stiff and it may be very difficult to hold them far enough away from the body to put them into the sleeves and legs.

> **Do not pull on the child's arms or legs in order to get his clothes on or off.**

If your baby has motor problems you may need to put him in the side-lying position and relax him before you can dress him (see page 60).

> Dressing any baby while he is in side-lying position can be helpful.

It will also help to have clothes that are easy to put on.

> Clothes that open all the way down the front or back are much easier to put over the head than those that don't and must be pulled over the head.

If you have some clothes that must be pulled over the head, you can make dressing easier by sewing a sheer nylon zipper in the front or back or by cutting the front open, binding the edges, and sewing velcro on the edges.

Many parents have found that loose or stretchable jumpsuits that zip up the front are the easiest to put on the baby.

The Easter Seal Society publishes a pamphlet titled, *Self Help Clothing for Handicapped Children*, Easter Seal Society, 2023 W. Ogden Ave., Chicago, IL 61612 that can be helpful.

Some special babies do not go stiff—they

ARE LIMP AS RAG DOLLS

It is difficult to make their arms and legs stay firm enough to put them into the arms and legs of clothes.

It helps if the clothes are somewhat loose and if the fabric stretches a little.

When your baby is three months old or more

it may be easier to sit him up and lean his body against yours while you are dressing him.

Sometimes the baby can control his muscles more when he is sitting up.

Putting the baby's head and arms into something like a tee shirt may be difficult.

Be careful that you do not bend his arms or turn his head in such a way that he will be uncomfortable.

Get clothes for your baby that are soft and flexible so he can move as much as possible.

If the clothes are stiff—like heavy denim—it will be even harder for you to dress your baby, and it will be harder for him to move after he is dressed. Some fabrics may irritate your baby's skin.

YOUR BABY MAY LIKE TO SLIP OFF HIS CLOTHES AND PLAY IN THE ALTOGETHER

Most babies do. It is more comfortable and they can move more easily when they are not wearing clothes.

You will probably not want your child to play outside in the altogether.

Although you may be embarrassed—your baby is not trying to attract attention.

He is only learning how to dress without help.

The first part of dressing is learning to undress.

Your baby will need to practice undressing before he will be ready to learn dressing.

Of course you won't want your baby undressing in public but it is important that he have a time to practice.

Just before bathtime and when changing to night clothes would be good times to practice undressing.

You may have to adjust your schedule to allow plenty of time to practice undressing when it is the proper time to do so.

Because it will take time for your baby to learn—maybe quite a long time—you may want to dress him during the day in clothes that are not easy to take off.

That way when you take him to a place where you can't watch him closely and where it would be embarrassing if he took his clothes off, you won't have to keep constant watch or worry.

Remember, if your baby is ready to practice—he will practice any where, any time.

Because it will probably take your special baby longer to learn to undress and dress, he will still need to practice when most children his age have already learned.

Try to be patient and allow him to practice. As he gets older you could supply some dress-up clothes for him to play with.

Jackets, hats, shoes, and pants that are large enough to slip on and off over the baby's other clothes
are good practice clothes—and fun, too.

Make sure that they are strong enough to take tugging and pulling **and that they are washable.**

LEARNING TO UNDRESS AND DRESS IS ONE OF THE IMPORTANT THINGS THAT YOUNG CHILDREN LEARN

4 SOME BABIES DO NOT USE THINGS LIKE OTHER BABIES

Instead of taking a toy out of the box and playing with it, the baby takes all the toys out of the
box then starts for
> the books on the shelf
> the kitchen cupboards
> the dresser drawers
> the clothes hamper
> and the . . .

He is not particularly interested in *using* any of these things

> Your baby is interested in taking things out of the place they are kept.

He is in fact, "using" the objects, but not in the usual sense.

Your baby may be looking to see how many things can fit in a drawer.

> He may be looking to see how much more space the toys can cover if they are taken out
> of the box where they are piled on top of each other and are spread across the floor
> **one at a time.**

Your baby may empty the wastebasket.

> He is not planning to make a mess; he is simply trying to see what is in the wastebasket.

> Some bright scraps of paper may look interesting to him.

> The wastebasket itself may look interesting to your baby and he may want to try
> wearing it as a hat—

> or using it as a car to push on the floor—

> or maybe see if the wastebasket is big enough to climb into.

Your special baby may like to
> **play with the leaves on the potted plants or**
> > **pound the piano keys with his teething ring or**
> > **chew the magazines on the coffee table and**
> > **pull on the drapes in the living room.**

It will be natural for you to run out of patience and lose your temper. You may even feel
hurt that your baby seems determined to destroy your things.

> *Although he may damage things, try to remember that he is not really trying to do so.*

YOUR BABY IS TRYING TO LEARN ABOUT THINGS

It will be wise to put your really good things away and make sure that the baby has some interesting things to play with (see page 119).

Babies who have trouble seeing, feeling, and understanding need to examine things more closely.

They may need to examine things that may not be interesting to other children—things like—

> the texture of a bowel movement
> how the pudding feels
> how the wall would look if touched with orange juice
> or how the wall would look if rubbed with a felt tip marker

EVENTUALLY YOU WILL WANT YOUR BABY TO LEARN TO

> **Keep all toys not being used in the toy box**
> **Leave things in cupboards and drawers**
> **Look at rather than eat potted plants**
> **Wipe the bowel movement away with tissue**
> and . . . and . . . and . . .

But in the beginning, he will need to examine these things by moving them around.

OF COURSE ALL BABIES LEARN THIS WAY—BUT YOUR SPECIAL BABY WILL TAKE LONGER TO LEARN

During that time he will be growing bigger and stronger and he may be able to reach some things that most babies can't while they are learning to understand things.

You may have to put away more things and put them away for a longer time.

Some parents have found that
> **certain things must be packed and**
> **certain things must be kept locked in**
> **cupboards and closets.**

SOME SPECIAL BABIES ARE VERY PERSISTENT ABOUT FINDING THEIR FAVORITE INTERESTING OBJECTS

If the favorite object is not an expensive one and it doesn't have sharp edges or parts that might be easily removed and put into the mouth, it might be wise to **allow your baby to play with it**.

Many babies like to play with a large assortment of things not usually considered toys.

old toasters (remove the cord)	plastic bottles and other containers
bath brushes	old slippers and shoes
egg beaters	magazines

HELP YOUR SPECIAL BABY LEARN TO TAKE CARE OF YOUR THINGS BY HELPING HIM LEARN TO TAKE CARE OF HIS THINGS

Have a special plce to keep his special objects

Since your baby will want to have things close at hand, **you may need to have several storage places**. One by his bed
one in the kitchen
one in the bathroom
one in the family room

Whenever the baby needs to interrupt his play for something else, **put the favorite object in the special place** where it is easy to see until he can return to play.

Some special babies will want to bathe and sleep with the favorite object.

If possible, let them. Gradually persuade the baby to put the special object on a stool or shelf near the tub or bed.

ALTHOUGH IT MAY SOUND LIKE A LONG PROCESS (AND IT IS), IT IS THE BEGINNING OF THE CHILD'S LEARNING TO TAKE CARE OF THINGS

VIII

No Two Babies Are Alike

EVEN BABIES WITH SIMILAR PROBLEMS
ARE DIFFERENT IN SOME WAYS

BUT CERTAIN CONDITIONS ARE MORE LIKELY
TO CAUSE SIMILAR PROBLEMS

1 IF YOUR BABY HAS ALLERGY PROBLEMS

He will probably have more skin irritations and be more nervous and sensitive.

He may have difficulty sleeping (see page 43) and more difficulty eating (see page 35).

Keeping track of exactly what he eats will be a very important part of taking care of your baby (see page 36).

He may be sensitive to certain materials and surfaces (see page 164).

He may suffer from diaper rash, rashes from bath soaps, and laundry soaps or detergents.

Sun and wind may irritate your baby's skin and so might skin lotions.

Your doctor will help you find the correct diet for your baby.

Ask your doctor about the diet suggestions for babies and children made by Dr. Smith (see page 35).

There will be many times when you feel sorry for your baby because he can't have candy, milk, orange juice, or the other foods that might cause an allergic reaction.

But try to remember that not eating these foods is best for him.

There are so many good things available to eat—look around and you will find something else that tastes good and will not bother your baby.

These same foods might be better for other family members too, because allergies tend to run in families. Often other family members are slightly allergic but not enough to cause a noticeable reaction.

There will also be times when you feel sorry for yourself *because it can be a real nuisance and sometimes an expense to be sure that your baby avoids the foods that will be harmful.*

It can be less of a nuisance if you serve the whole family foods that do not bother your baby.

It is sometimes possible to improve the health of the entire family by taking care of the baby's allergies.

It is also wise to have the baby tested to see if he is bothered by family pets, certain fabrics, or plants.

2 SOME BABIES HAVE BRAIN DAMAGE

This means that the brain was injured by lack of oxygen or blood circulation, or infection, or by direct physical injury to the brain.

The results could range from a few cells that don't function well to almost complete inability to learn to think and move.

Generally speaking, babies with brain damage
> are more bothered by noises, lights, and changes in routine.

> They seem to notice changes in temperature and little changes in the way they are handled.

> They tend to have more muscle and movement difficulties.

Their acute sensitivity makes their care extra difficult because they are prone to be fussy if someone other than the usual caregiver tries to take care of them (see page 63).

You will want to be sure that routines are as consistent as possible but, at the same time, it is important that the baby learn to let others handle him.

Your baby will also be very sensitive to the way *you* feel.
> If you are upset, the baby will be upset.

Try to be calm and respond to his sensitivity in a matter-of-fact way. He will be more calm if you make sure that you feed him frequently and that the foods do not cause rashes or increased restlessness.

Occupational and physical therapists can help you learn how to handle the baby.

Special teachers can show you how to help the baby learn.

It will be difficult to be calm when your baby fusses so much and there will be times when you want to fuss, too—
> **but don't when you are with your baby.**

> *Have someone that you trust take care of the baby and get away from time-to-time.*

If there is no one in your family available, you may want to trade off baby sitting with another parent of a special child.

CALM PARENTS ARE THE GREATEST ASSET THAT A BRAIN DAMAGED CHILD CAN HAVE

3   YOUR BABY MAY HAVE CEREBRAL PALSY

This is sometimes called **spastic**.

Cerebral palsy means that the central nervous system is not functioning adequately.

Sometimes it is possible to help the child learn how to organize the central nervous system by carefully moving his body and helping the baby learn to move. (See Motor Problems, page 53).

It may be hard for you to see that the baby is not moving like other babies. People who have worked with many babies, however, can see that your baby is not learning how to hold his head up or move his hips and shoulders separately or put weight on his hands and knees.

HELPING THE BABY LEARN TO MOVE CORRECTLY WHEN THE BABY IS VERY YOUNG IS IMPORTANT

Do not wait for him to "outgrow" the stiffness or the problems of not being able to hold his head up and turn over.

If you do, instead of getting better, your baby will probably get worse.

Babies with cerebral palsy will have motor problems (see page 53).

Your's will probably be hard to dress and bathe (see pages 152 and 163).

He will have special difficulties eating (see page 29).

If it is hard for the baby to move his mouth, have someone observe the way he swallows to see if the baby has tongue thrust. Learn how to feed him if he does push the tongue out rather than push it along the top of the mouth in order to swallow.

You may also need to have some special chairs or other equipment to help hold your baby in a good position for eating.

A physical or occupational therapist can tell you what kind of equipment you need. Many of them will be able to build the equipment for you.

If your baby has trouble moving his mouth, he may need some equipment to help him learn to communicate. Sometimes the baby can learn to communicate by using pictures of a glass of milk, the toilet, the family pet, and the family members. You can then ask questions, such as, "Do you want a drink?" and the child can answer by touching or looking at the picture of a glass of milk.

Taking care of your child will be physically tiring. Show others how to handle the baby so you can get away now and then. You might volunteer some of your respite time to help other parents with their special children. But, remember to help yourself, too, by **taking a nap or a bubble bath**.

4 SOME SPECIAL BABIES HAVE CYSTIC FIBROSIS

If your baby does, he will have special difficulties breathing, choke easily, and often have bulky, sticky, bad smelling stools (diaper mess).

Sometimes will be worse than others.

It is important not to become excited and to react as calmly as possible.

But it is also important to get the help the baby needs.

Sometimes it will be necessary to have the lungs cleared out. A respiration therapist can show you how to help drain the fluid out of the lungs.

Your baby may need special medication.

He may need special food that will help keep the mucous from becoming too thick.

Sometimes your baby will be extra tired and need more rest than usual.

Other times he will feel lively and happy.

It is important to be cheerful and try to enjoy the happy times with your baby.

And it is equally important to be calm when the times are more difficult.

It is only human for you to be upset and angry or feel like crying when you see your baby uncomfortable and when he coughs so much.

You must try your hardest to keep your tears from the baby because if he becomes upset and cries, the problem gets worse.

There are pamphlets and other material available from the Cystic Fibrosis Association.

These may help you learn to help your baby without spoiling or pampering him.

5 DENTAL AND ORAL PROBLEMS

In the beginning of development the mouth and nose are not separated, they comprise one large opening.

Some babies are born without a separation between the mouth and nose.
>A doctor or an oral surgeon would call this *cleft palate* and *cleft lip* if the space between the nostrils on the face was also open.

Without a separation between the mouth and nose it is very difficult for the baby to learn to suck and swallow.
>There are several nipples that have been designed to help the baby nurse. Your doctor will help you find a medical supply house that has the proper nipple for your baby. It may be that you will need to experiment with several designs before you find one that works.

If your baby has this problem, it will almost always be necessary for the baby to have surgery to close the space between the nose and mouth and to construct tissue between the nostrils if that is missing, too. Usually the repair is done in a series of operations.

Because having this work done will help your baby in eating and learning to make sounds, the doctor will probably suggest that it be started when the baby is very young.
>Just how young will depend upon how difficult it is for your baby to eat and how strong he is.

Every parent worries about surgery for infants, but this surgery has been done for many years and the results are usually very good. Remember, too, the baby will look better and be better able to eat and talk.
>The doctor can probably tell you about other babies who have had the surgery if you would like to talk to their parents.

Most of these children will also need the help of a speech therapist who has special interest and training in working with babies who have had this kind of problem. Check with the American Speech, Language, and Hearing Association, 10801 Rockville Pike, Rockville, MD 20852, if there is not a speech clinic in your area.

There are other problems that babies sometimes have with the formation of their mouths.
>Teeth may not be fastened to other structures and they develop in straight or crooked formations in the mouth.

>The teeth of special babies are frequently not in the usual place. Sometimes the baby will have a tooth grow out of the top or the side of the mouth. Sometimes he will have two teeth that grow together. It will probably be necessary to have an x-ray to find exactly where the teeth are and what kinds of things can be done to help make the baby's mouth most functional.

>Since the mouth and each set of teeth are unique, it will be necessary to have help for your baby that is designed by a specialist who understands the mouth and teeth and has experience working on dental restoration of infants.

Some medications (see page 41) can cause the gums to enlarge and hang over or protrude from the teeth. Sometimes it is possible to switch to another medication that will produce the desired benefit without the unpleasant side-effect but sometimes it is necessary to put up with side-effects because that medication is the only one that controls the other problems the baby has.

6 YOU MAY BE TOLD THAT YOUR BABY IS DEVELOPMENTALLY DELAYED OR DELAYED

That means that he will be slower learning and doing things than other babies and he will also be slower growing.

It is important that you make sure your baby has plenty of opportunity to see things and do things and to meet people.

Take him to the park, the zoo, and the grocery store (see page 72).

Have some durable, interesting toys for your baby to explore and have some good places inside and out where your baby can play (see page 124).

Invite the neighborhood children over to play. Take your baby to a nursery school from time-to-time.

Help him learn to share with other children. There are songs about sharing and taking turns in the Socialization album (see page 117).

Talk to your baby about the things you are doing (see page 136).

Listen and respond to him when he tries to talk—even if he doesn't talk clearly enough for you to understand. Try to guess what your baby is wanting to say and answer as if you understand (see page 148).

"Read" stories to him that have plenty of pictures. Make up stories for your baby using pictures of him and pictures of the other family members (see page 13).

Have a place where your baby can climb on swings, slides, old innertubes, and steps. Encourage him to try riding a tricycle, pushing a big truck, and pulling a wagon.

From time-to-time you will be embarrassed because your child may be as large and as old as children who can ride trikes or bikes but your child may still be playing with pull toys.

Try not to be embarrassed. The important thing is to be sure that your child is learning what he is ready to learn. Enjoy that learning with your child. Sometimes things that come slowly can be appreciated even more.

7 DIABETES MELLITUS

The body changes food into a special sugar called glucose. In order to use this sugar the body must have insulin.

Your baby's body may not be able to make insulin or it may be able to make insulin, but not as much as the baby needs.

The problem is called diabetes mellitus or sugar diabetes.

If there is no insulin in the cells of the body, the body cannot use the glucose (or sugar) properly and it is expelled from the body as waste.

One of the first signs of diabetes is that there is a large amount of urine.
The person then starts to drink a large amount of water or other liquid.
Then the person begins to eat large amounts of food, but still loses weight.

If nothing is done to correct this condition the person may lapse into a diabetic coma.

It may take a few weeks for all of these symptoms to appear, **so be alert for any of them**.

Have the doctor test the urine and decide if other tests are needed.

If your baby has this problem it can be treated. Your doctor can teach you to become a "mini physician" so that you can learn how much of what kinds of foods the baby should eat, how much insulin he needs, and how to tell when he needs to have more insulin or more food.

When he is moving around a lot, he will use more energy and use it more quickly so he will need more food and more insulin than he will when he is inactive and quiet.

It will be necessary for your doctor to plan the baby's diet carefully and to show you how to give him insulin.

Later, when the child gets older, you and the doctor will help your child learn to measure the food and give the insulin.

Of course you will be upset if your baby has this problem, but if you and the baby learn to take care of the food and insulin balance, your child will not have to lead a handicapped life—just because he has diabetes.

If one member of the family has diabetes, it is more likely that other members will, also. You should be alert for the warning signs.

8 YOUR BABY MAY HAVE A DISLOCATED HIP

Sometimes babies are born with the leg bone not quite in the hip socket.

The hip socket grows and develops as the baby bears weight on the joint.

If your child is not able to move around or if his legs are very spastic or high tone (see Motor Problems, page 54), the hip socket may not develop properly and the leg bone may be pulled away from the socket.

There may be some therapy or exercises that can help the socket develop.

Your baby may need surgery to help develop the socket.

You may need to have the baby put in a cast to help the hip grow better.

For each of these situations you will need a therapist and an orthopedist who is familiar with congenital problems of babies to show you how to hold and take care of your child, and to guide you in the best medical treatment.

You will probably feel uncomfortable and even afraid handling your baby.

It is important for you to get over that feeling so that you can care for him, play with him, and take him out to see things.

The more you handle your baby, the more comfortable you will be about the dislocated hip.

Show others how to handle your baby—he needs to learn to know and trust others, and you need to have a break from always arranging your life around your baby's.

Sometimes the child's hip socket develops enough so he no longer has the problem and other times the dislocated hip is something that persists throughout life. Sometimes, what makes the difference is how soon something is done to help the baby.

9 YOUR BABY MAY HAVE DOWN SYNDROME

Another name for Down syndrome is mongolism, because it was thought that the eyes of Down syndrome babies were shaped like the eyes of oriental peoples.

The medical term, Down syndrome, was given in the 1800s. It was named after Dr. Landon Down who first described the affected babies.

Because it is possible to see that a baby has Down syndrome by the look of the eyes, the shape of the head, the size of the ears, and a number of other things, your doctor probably told you in the delivery room or soon after and explained that your baby would have learning problems.

Your baby will have some difficulties, but probably fewer than the doctor thought.

Educators who have been working with Down syndrome children have found that if the baby has a lot of attention, he can learn more than was thought to be possible.

Many Down syndrome babies have heart problems. Most of these can be successfully corrected by surgery when the children are quite young.

If your baby has a heart problem and your doctor is not a surgeon or specialist, he can refer you to one.

Down syndrome babies frequently have difficulty breathing and other respiratory problems.

Especially if your climate is dry, a cold water humidifier running in the baby's bedroom all the time may help keep him from becoming congested.

Most Down syndrome babies are quiet, pleasant, and loving. You may think that your baby does not enjoy having you talk and play with him because he may not look right back at you and coo and smile.

It is important to keep talking and smiling and to give the baby plenty of time to get ready to smile and coo back. It will take your baby longer to know what you are doing and to get ready to coo and smile back to you.

In fact, the time that it takes to learn is the biggest problem for Down syndrome babies . . . they need more time to learn to hold the head up and move. (See Motor Problems, page 53).
they need more time to learn to smile and talk (see Language Problems, page 136).
they need more time to learn to dress and undress (see page 163).
they need more time to learn to feed themselves (see page 31).
they will probably be older than other children are when they are ready to be toilet trained (see page 155).

But Down syndrome babies are not slow to learn how to **show their affection to those who care for them.**

If you hug your baby and take care of him lovingly, you will find that he will learn to show care and affection for you—and his teddy bear—and other people who are warm and outgoing.

IN FACT, THE BEST WAY TO TEACH YOUR BABY ANYTHING IS TO LET HIM WATCH YOU DO IT

Then let the baby try even if he is clumsy in the beginning and continues to be clumsy for a long time.

Eventually your baby will learn to do things just about the way you do things.

He will learn to put toys away—*If you put your things away*

He will learn to eat neatly—*If you eat neatly*

He will learn to like and respect people—*If you like and respect people*

Your baby will also learn from other babies and children. Arrange for him to be with babies and children who do not have special problems as much as possible.

In an article in *We Have Been There*, Publisher's Press, Salt Lake City, Utah, Pat Vyas tells how she sent her Down syndrome son to a regular nursery school.

It will undoubtedly bother you from time-to-time to contrast your special baby with other babies the same age who can do more things than your's can. Sometimes you will feel like crying—crying because your baby is missing things, and crying because, as a parent, you seem to be missing the joy of seeing the baby develop like other babies. If you cry around your baby, he will probably wipe your eyes and give you a hug.

The article by Carol Michaelis in *The Exceptional Parent* of February, 1974, tells how one mother felt about her Down syndrome son. A second article in *The Exceptional Parent,* December, 1976, "Merry Christmas, Jim, and Happy Birthday," tells about some mixed feelings.

The book by Marci Hanson, *Teaching Your Down's Syndrome Infant*, published by University Park Press (1977) gives suggestions on how to teach your Down syndrome child.

10 YOUR BABY MAY HAVE A SEIZURE DISORDER OR EPILEPSY

Sometimes it is said that the baby has **convulsions**, if the seizures are characterized by rigidity and jerking of the arms, legs, and body.

Generally speaking there are three kinds of seizures

One in which the whole body goes rigid and jerks, and the victim falls to the ground.

Another is a brief moment when the person seems to "black out" and sometimes moves the head in a nodding fashion.

A third is when just part of the body, one side, goes rigid or jerks.

Other types of convulsions can occur and special help is needed to determine whether or not they are really seizures.

Seizures can be very frightening—they frighten most people—and if **your baby** *has seizures, you will be even more frightened.*

You will probably be afraid that the baby might hurt himself during the seizure.

And you might be afraid that he might sustain brain damage because of the seizure.

Seizures that are not controlled and recur over a long period can cause brain damage.

Sometimes they happen because there is a brain problem or because of poor metabolism in the baby's body that needs medical attention.

If a baby has a high fever he may have a convulsion
although nothing else is wrong.

Some babies have seizures with or without fever.

If your child has a convulsion—fever or no fever—it is important to have the doctor see the baby. If they are recurring seizures, he will need appropriate medical treatment.

Because the doctor will not actually see the seizure, it is important that you describe exactly what the baby did and how long he continued to do it.

The doctor will only be able to treat the baby if you can carefully describe what happened.

Tell the doctor whether the baby's arm and leg on one side only jerked, or if the movements were on both sides of the body, or if the baby was pulled backward or forward.

Watch the clock so you can tell about how long it lasts.

Most seizures last from a few seconds to one or two minutes.

If your baby has one seizure after another and the entire duration is more than five minutes, call the doctor. Tell the nurse it is an emergency, explain why, and the doctor will probably want to see you right away.

Page 2 tells more about keeping a record of seizures and reporting them to your doctor.

Brief seizures can be more difficult to treat but often they can be controlled and every effort to control them should be made.

It is important that you and your baby have the help of a pediatrician or a neurologist who has a special interest in epilepsy. Call the doctor's office and ask if the doctor has a special interest in epilepsy.

You might be able to find someone with special interest through the Epilepsy Foundation of America, 1828 L Street NW, Washington, D.C. 20036. The foundation has other information that might be helpful to you and your family.

Try to remain calm.

It will be difficult and you will worry that the baby will have another seizure.

You could make that anticipation the focus of your life—you could teach the baby to measure life from one seizure to another.

In order to learn and grow, your baby will need to do as many things as possible, in the same way that all children do.

Try to treat your child's seizures as a matter-of-fact occurrence. If he is tired after the seizure, let him rest.

If the child is not tired, let him continue what he was doing before the seizure.

Explain the situation to grandparents and friends so they won't be alarmed—and so they won't treat the baby as if he were sickly.

The child who has seizures is not sick.

A seizure is caused because of an abnormal amount of electrical energy in the brain for a few seconds that causes the child to behave differently.

You and your baby can become emotionally exhausted if you treat each seizure as a crisis point in your lives.

You can help prevent your child's seizures by giving the prescribed medication regularly—without missing doses, by keeping your baby as healthy as possible, by making sure that he sleeps and eats at regular times and gets fresh air and exercise, and by taking special care when the baby is sick.

Babies run fever very easily.

If your baby has a high fever (see page 11), reduce it as quickly as possible.

Of course you wish that your baby did not have problems with seizures and sometimes you will become discouraged and feel like crying. Be careful that you do not cry when the baby is with you. He is unaware that anything has happened when a seizure occurs and to see people frightened because of something he apparently did, but doesn't know about, can be very upsetting to him.

11 YOUR SPECIAL BABY MAY HAVE HEARING PROBLEMS

He might be called hearing impaired, hard-of-hearing, or deaf.

Many special babies have hearing problems. It could be your baby's major problem, or it might be one of many others.

If your baby does not look at you when you talk to him, jump when there is a loud noise, or like toys that make music, he may have a hearing problem.

It is important to have his hearing tested by an audiologist who has special equipment.

Most school audiologists test hearing by putting earphones on the child and having the child hold up a finger when he hears a noise.

Special babies cannot be tested this way.

If your baby has a hearing problem in the outer ear, a hearing aid may help.

If the hearing problem is in the inner ear, a hearing aid won't help.

If the audiologist tells you that there is a problem, have him determine the need for a hearing aid and help you get it fitted.

Many hearing aid salesmen know a great deal about the aid but very little about how to fit it.

A poorly fitting aid does not help the child hear better and it can be a real nuisance.

Make sure that your child does not have ear infections.

Many special babies who do not coo, smile, or cry much cannot feel that they hurt. It is possible for the baby to have severe ear problems and not fuss about it.

Other times the baby will cry, fuss, and hold his ears or not sleep and eat well.

Many Down syndrome babies (see page 178) don't fuss at all when they have ear infections.

If your baby has trouble hearing, he will have trouble learning language.

Much of what the baby learns to say is what he hears other people saying.

It will be important for you to be sure that the baby can see you whenever you want him to understand you.

Help him understand by showing him and by gesturing to him.

Be sure that your facial expression tells the baby what you want him to know.

As the child grows older it sometimes helps to teach him signs for words and ideas.

If your baby does not hear well or does not at all, be sure to have a teacher who is trained in working with hearing-impaired children see your baby and show you how to work with him.

These organizations may help you: Tracy Clinic, San Francisco; Alexander Graham Bell Association for the Deaf, 3417 Volta Place, NE, Washington, D.C. 20007; and National Association for the Deaf, 814 Thayer Avenue, Silver Spring, MD 20910.

There will be times when you feel angry because you cannot make your baby understand you.

There will be times when you are sad because your baby can't hear your favorite music.

There will be times when you feel that your child is left out because he cannot talk to other children.

It will be natural for you to feel these ways—you probably will again and again. It may help to have someone to talk to. Sometimes it helps to talk to another parent, a counselor, or a clergyman. Don't be frustrated if they don't seem to understand what is bothering you, you may not know exactly what is bothering you, but the act of talking in itself will make you feel better.

Try to remember that parents of children without hearing difficulties are sometimes frustrated when they try to communicate with their children.

Arrange to go shopping, for a walk, or do something that you enjoy, so you can come back refreshed and ready to enjoy being with your child.

A child can learn language faster from a parent who enjoys talking to the child (see Language Problems, page 136).

12   YOUR BABY MAY HAVE HEART PROBLEMS

If your baby has a heart murmur, heart damage, or a heart defect, he will need special care.

It will be important that he does not move and run so much that his heart cannot pump the blood fast enough.

It will be hard to tell exactly how much your baby can do.

You will want to keep him from doing so much that his face turns blue or that his lips and fingernails turn blue.

Yet you will not want to keep your baby from being with others and doing things with them any more than is necessary.

Each activity will need to be examined and evaluated separately.

There will be days when the baby feels good enough to be active and days when he does not.

If the baby has a cold, you will need to be extra careful.

Some types of heart conditions can be corrected or at least improved by surgery. Often medications can help the heart function better.

You may want the opinion of more than one doctor

Babies with Down syndrome (see page 178) frequently have heart conditions that can be corrected by surgery.

Despite the fact that if your baby has heart problems, it is important to have play time.

You may want a play area nearby so you can supervise easily (see pages 124-125).

Thinking about the heart problem can cause you to worry.

If you worry and worry, the baby will feel the tension and be less relaxed and less able to enjoy exploring as much as possible.

If you have some quiet activities—such as music, stories, miniature cars, soldiers, or trains to play with your child can be happy and interested even during the times when he needs to be less physically active.

13 YOUR BABY MAY HAVE HEMOPHILIA

Persons with hemophilia have blood that coagulates slowly and they bleed very easily.

Not only do they bleed from breaks in the skin but they may have bleeding inside—as other people do—but the internal bleeding can be a major problem because it doesn't stop.

If your baby bleeds enough, he will need a blood transfusion.

There is medication that can be given to help the blood coagulate.

It is also important that your baby not get bumps or bruises that may cause internal bleeding.

It will be even more important for you to be sure that he has **a safe place to play** (see pages 113 and 124) and that you keep an eye on him while he is playing.

You may want to talk to parents and select playmates who are fun but not rough in their play.

Invite these children to come play with your child.

It will be very tricky to be sure that your baby is not bumped or bruised yet gets the regular experiences of childhood, since bumps and bruises are so much a part of growing up.

*Since hemophilia is inherited from the mother, it is especially easy for her to feel guilty about the baby's problems—***don't***—it's not your fault. After all, you inherited the ability to pass it on from your parents, and so on—It's not really much different than members of a family having red hair or blue eyes—***it just feels different!***

14 YOUR BABY MAY HAVE HYDROCEPHALUS

This means that the fluid that is naturally in the brain ventricles does not drain and can cause the skull to become enlarged and the brain to be damaged. It is sometimes called water on the brain.

Babies with spina bifida, myelomeningocele or meningocele usually have some difficulty with normal drainage of fluid from the brain ventricles.

Some babies with cerebral palsy also have difficulty with fluid drainage.

Sometimes the baby needs *a shunt* to correct hydrocephalus.

Many areas of the body produce a water-like fluid which collects in certain spaces—the eyes, the kidneys, the stomach and intestines, and the brain. The fluid spaces in the brain are called ventricles. Fluid is constantly produced in the ventricles. It passes outside the brain, bathes the brain and spinal cord, and then it is taken up by the bloodstream through special little valves on the surface of the brain. If passage of this fluid is blocked, it causes pressure to build up—like water in a balloon.

There is no room in the brain ventricles to store the fluid unless they enlarge, causing the baby's head to enlarge. The fluid can crowd the brain and other structures in the baby's head. It is possible to insert a small plastic tube in the body to drain the fluid away from the head area. This tube is called a *shunt*. A shunt can drain the extra fluid from the delicate brain area to the stomach area. It is much easier for the body to dispose of the extra fluid from the stomach area. The placing of a shunt is a rather simple procedure. It needs to be done when the infant is *very* young to prevent the buildup of fluid from enlarging the baby's head.

The plastic tube is placed just under the skin and a slight ridge is visible at the back of the neck where the shunt is. You should not place anything tight around the area or push or rub on it, however it is not necessary to be overly cautious or protective. The baby can take an ordinary bath, swim, and engage in other activities with the family.

Sometimes the shunt doesn't work well and another needs to be put in place, but usually the shunt works for years. Frequently, as the baby gets older and the shunt relieves the early pressure, the condition improves and is no longer a problem.

If your baby has a shunt, and his behavior changes suddenly—becomes very irritable, cries like he is in pain, or starts vomiting for no apparent reason—call your doctor.

15 YOUR CHILD MAY HAVE HYPOTHYROIDISM

In order to be active and alert the body must have *thyroxine*.

If your baby's body does not produce enough, he may be slow and listless, have difficulty staying awake to nurse, and generally have *low tone* (see page 54).

The baby's skin may be dry; he may be constipated, and may have trouble learning to roll over and sit up.

If the thyroid gland does not produce the necessary amount of thyroxine, it is called *hypo* (low) thyroidism.

If the thyroid deficiency began before birth, the baby will be slow in growth, mental development, and sexual development.

This condition is called *cretinism*.

Sometimes it is hard to tell for sure if an infant is Down syndrome (see page 178) or has thyroid problems.

Your doctor can test the thyroid function to decide if the baby needs to be given thyroxine.

If your baby has hypothyroidism, thyroxine can help him develop. How much the thyroxin can help will depend on how long the baby has had a thyroid deficiency.

The problem can start before the baby is born or it can start in childhood. It can even begin in adulthood.

If your child slowly or suddenly becomes listless, you will want to tell your doctor about your concerns.

16   YOUR BABY MAY HAVE MALFORMATIONS

Sometimes during pregnancy certain parts of the body do not grow
as they should and they are *malformed.*

It is not unusual for babies to have extra fingers or toes and some babies are born without hands or arms and some without feet or legs.

Sometimes, too, the openings for elimination of urine and bowel waste are malformed.

From time to time babies are born with extra nipples on other parts of the body or undeveloped sex organs and it is difficult to tell if the baby is a boy or a girl.

There can also be malformations of the brain.

Depending on which part is not developed, the baby may experience many or few problems in growing, learning, and developing.

If there are many problems or if the problems relate to vital life processes like breathing, eating, or elimination, your baby may need immediate surgery or treatment in order to live.

There are many adults who were born with missing or malformed body parts.

Your doctor can help you find someone who has a problem that is similar to the problems your child has. Or you might contact: National Foundation—March of Dimes, 1275 Mamaroneck Ave., White Plains, NY 10605, or Easter Seal Society for Crippled Children and Adults, 2023 W. Ogden Ave., Chicago, IL 60612.

Sometimes it helps to be able to talk with another parent or an adult who has grown up with the disability.

These societies might also help you find a doctor who has a special interest in birth defects and malformations. Sometimes surgery, therapy, or artificial limbs can help your baby. Each child will have different needs because the exact location and extent of the problem vary.

17 IF YOUR BABY'S HEAD IS VERY SMALL, HE MAY HAVE MICROCEPHALUS.

When the baby is born, bones of the head are beside each other in the proper position but they have not grown together. As the baby grows, the bones expand and grow, too. When the heads gets to full size, the bones grow together.

The bones in a baby's head usually don't finish growing together until the baby is about two years old.

The bones in some babies heads grow together when they are younger. In some babies the bones have grown together before they are born, and before the brain and other skull areas have completely developed.
This does not leave room for proper development. This makes the head small—a condition called *microcephalus*.

If the baby has microcephalus, it will be difficult for him to learn—he will need to have the same things happen over and over again before he can remember them.

He will need to see the same thing over and over again before he can remember it.

There is no way to help the head grow once the bones of the head have grown together.

Sometimes it is thought that radiation or some injury may have caused the condition, but the reasons are not known.

Babies with cerebral palsy sometimes have microcephaly.

If your baby has microcephaly and does not have cerebral palsy or other injuries, you may want to discuss the situation with a genetic counselor.

18 MUSCULAR DYSTROPHY MAY BE A PROBLEM FOR YOUR BABY

Muscular dystrophy means that the muscles begin to get weak and can no longer support the body, because of a specific disease of the muscles.

Parents usually notice their child at about three years becomes clumsy and awkward. Kindergarten teachers notice when the child falls frequently. Because muscular dystrophy is usually inherited, parents are usually aware that the baby might develop the problem. It is possible to test for the condition even before symptoms are evident.

Male children inherit the condition that eventually causes the muscles to become weak and the muscle tissue to be replaced with fat. Occasionally a girl has the condition but it is usually carried through female members of the family and only the male members are affected.

Although diets, vitamins, and therapy have been tried, none of them seems to be effective. Group games that encourage movement and deep breathing are more effective than having the child lie still while the therapist or parent moves the body through passive exercises.

If some male children in your family have had this problem, you will probably be worried about your child—and so will the rest of the family.

Although it helps to be aware of the possibility and to watch for some sign that the baby is having difficulty,
constant worry will not help the baby or you.

Maintenance of proper health and nutrition can be important. If the child overeats, the danger of having fatty tissue replace muscle tissue is greater than if the child eats an appropriate diet that includes plenty of fresh fruits and vegetables. It is also helpful to get routine rest and sleep.

Medical tests in some types of muscular dystrophy can identify carriers. Genetic counseling can be important to your family.

The most important thing that you can do for your baby is to

Enjoy your child

Take time for reading, simple games, and songs, and enjoying family holidays.

Mothers, especially will worry about their sons
and feel badly because they feel responsible.

But you are *not* "responsible".

You could be the carrier and pass the condition on to your sons,
but you did not do that purposely.

You received the condition from your parents who in turn did not

choose to have it but received it from their parent.

If the condition does run in your family, you have probably known about it all your life.

Fathers and fathers' families may be disappointed and angry.
It may be difficult to know how to deal with that anger without directing it to the mother and rejecting the son.

Counseling may help. The Muscular Dystrophy Association, 810 Seventh Ave., New York, NY 10019 has printed materials that may be interesting to you.

They also have community services available and can assist in getting some treatment without cost and some equipment such as wheelchairs and lifts.

19 YOUR BABY MAY HAVE MYELOMENINGOCELE, MENINGOCELE, OR SPINA BIFIDA

These are caused because the spinal canal did not develop completely.

In myelomeningocele the spinal cord protrudes through the bony structure.

In meningocele the covering of the spinal cord comes through the bony structure.

In spina bifida there is a bony defect but tissue does not protrude.

In the first 30 days of fetal development, a tube forms that later holds the brain stem and spinal cord. The tube in your baby did not develop completely.

The cause of the developmental problem is unknown.

If your baby has myelomeningocele, the legs and lower parts of the body will have weak muscles and they will not be strong enough to hold your child up without some kind of support.

It will be difficult for your child to learn to walk and use the toilet, because the muscles will be so weak that opening and closing the bowel and bladder may not be possible. It is important to have some help very early so you can help the baby empty the bowel and bladder completely to prevent infection.

Sometimes it is necessary for the baby to have medication to keep the waste material soft.

Your baby will probably have hydrocephalus (see page 186) and may need to have the extra fluid drained from the brain with a shunt.

Sometimes surgery will be recommended to try to straighten the hip or legs so the child can stand up. The surgery can be expensive.

Be careful not to allow your child to soothe himself by eating. If the child has too much food to digest, there will be more elimination problems. If the child is overweight it will be more difficult for him to move around.

Of course you will feel badly if your child cannot learn to stand and walk and run like other babies. You will probably become tired of dealing with the baby's elimination problems. Take some time to cry about it and take some time to get away from your child's problems. But try not to blame the child or yourself for the conditions. No one is to blame—the condition is just there.

20 OSTEOGENESIS IMPERFECTA MEANS IMPERFECT BONE FORMATION

If your baby has this condition, the bones will be small and easily broken. The baby has a general protein deficiency and the bones are curved and the teeth decay easily. Hearing is a problem because the bones of the inner ear are not formed properly.

Sometimes the condition can be treated with specialized foods and minerals, but this treatment has not been too effective. The curved long bones can sometimes be straightened by having a steel rod inserted. This can help stabilize the bones and keep them from being so fragile.

If your baby has osteogenesis imperfecta, his bones will break easily so he should not be allowed to participate in activities where he might fall or get bumped.

Keeping your child protected and still not limiting activities too much will be a real challenge.

If your child is interested in a certain toy or activity, it might be wise to help find a way for him to enjoy it rather than make a scene about forbidding it.

A carpeted floor or a protected play area could make things more safe.

The condition is inherited and may run in your family.

If the baby inherited the problem from you, it will be easy for you to feel guilty.

You are not responsible for your child's problem.

You did not choose to have the condition in your family and neither did other family members.

Try to deal with the situation as wisely and calmly as possible.

Children with osteogenesis imperfecta can grow up to be bridge and chess champions and violin virtuosos.

Just because it is wise to avoid participating in physical activities does not mean that the child should avoid participating in intellectual activities.

You may want to read the book by Beverly Plummer, a mother of a child with osteogenesis imperfecta, *Give Everyday a Chance*, New York, G. P. Putman & Sons, 1970.

21 YOUR BABY MAY HAVE PKU (PHENYLKETONURIA) OR OTHER METABOLIC DISORDERS

The body usually gets the nutrients that it needs by breaking down or metabolizing foods during digestion. For some people the breaking down process doesn't work as well as it does for other people. Those people are not able to get the energy they need and thus growth is threatened.

If your baby has PKU he will have difficulty metabolizing proteins so they can be used in the body.

Other babies may have difficulty breaking down sugars in milk. (galactosemia).

And other babies will have difficulty with other foods.

If your baby has one of these problems it is very important that you do not feed him the problem foods and be sure that no one else feeds these foods to him.

Not only are the foods not useable for your baby but they can actually be a *poison* to the baby's system.

There are special diets that can be given to your baby so that he can have the energy necessary for growth and development without having the foods that can be harmful to the baby's body.

The diet will be a nuisance and the extra foods may stretch your budget.

Feeding them, however, will be worth the expense. Usually, as the babies grow, they become able to handle regular foods.

You may think the foods are tasteless, but to your baby they won't be.

If your baby has never tasted spices and flavorings, he will not miss them.
Those spices and flavorings are probably not part of the food that is really valuable, even to adults.

Try to make mealtime cheerful and pleasant for your baby and you. (Having some of your favorite music playing may be helpful.)

When you take the baby out, pack some of the special foods—just in case—even if you don't plan to be out past feeding time.

22 YOUR BABY MAY HAVE SCOLIOSIS

This means that the spinal vertebra are curved to one side. This is because part of the bones of the spine are not formed properly. It can also be caused by neuromuscular problems in cerebral palsy, or muscle problems associated with muscular dystrophy, or as the result of polio. Some children develop a curve when they reach their teen years and the cause is not known.

In most cases it is not possible to straighten the curve that is there, but by keeping the body flexible through exercising the trunk area it is possible to keep the condition from getting more servere.

A physical therapist can show you what movements your baby needs to be making

to help straighten the trunk muscles and make it possible for him to move his hips and shoulders separately.

After you know what movements are helpful, you can move the baby that way several times a day and help him learn to move that way.

Sometimes bracing helps prevent more curving, but usually the brace is only used for older children who exercise inside the brace and exercise when they are not wearing the brace.

You will become bored with the exercises—and so will your baby.

It will be easier for both of you if you make them into a game and if you learn to enjoy the time that you spend together.

You may want to make a note on the calendar or keep another record of some kind to help you remember to do the exercises again and again, day after day.

The exercise routine in the evening could be part of the Dad's play time with the baby.

You may be depressed and sad about the way that your baby's spine looks, and you will probably need to feel bad and sorry for your baby, but don't let the baby know it. It will be difficult for your baby to even see his back. It is important that your baby like his own body, so don't discuss the curve or show how sorry you feel about it. When the child is older he may want to see it. Show him with the mirror and explain it—but not over and over again.

23 YOUR BABY MAY BE SPASTIC

This means that the muscles are pulled tightly.

That keeps the body straight, the toes pointed, and the head tipped back. The arms and legs are difficult to bend. Because of this stiffness it is not possible for the baby to move the body to reach things or do things.

It will be difficult to dress and feed your baby and it will be difficult for him to learn to move and play.

Spasticity is one type of cerebral palsy, and can be treated by using special movement patterns that a physical or occupational therapist can show you. They can also show you how to pick up your baby and hold him. Generally it is necessary to bend the arms and legs to keep the body from being stiff.

The book by Nancy Finnie, *Handling the Young Cerebral Palsied Child at Home*, gives a variety of excellent suggestions for equipment and handling.

Naturally you will feel badly that your baby cannot move freely. The only way to help your baby is to continually help him move in the proper way.

Plan to have someone help you with the baby's movement from time-to-time.

Movement practice is a good thing for dad to include in his play time with the baby.

24 YOUR BABY MAY HAVE VISION PROBLEMS

Sometimes this might be called partially sighted.

It may be hard for you to tell for sure whether your baby can see.

It may be hard for *anyone* to tell for sure whether your baby can see or how much he sees.

The professionals are not trying to put you off. It is very difficult to tell how much one can see because seeing is partly something that the eyes do and partly something that the brain does.

When babies are very young and have not had much time to learn they cannot tell if what is in front of them is something for them to see or not. It might just look like a blur.

Only by looking and looking can the baby learn that the blur is the same all the time.

If your baby is having some trouble seeing and some trouble understanding what he sees, it will be more difficult to tell how much he *can* see.

Almost everyone can to some degree— Some people only see light and dark

or shades of light and dark. But they can see objects as they move—they may not see the colors, but they can see the shadow moving.

Even if you think that your baby cannot see well, you should show him things and talk to him while you do. Get toys for your baby that are not only bright and pretty but that have parts that will move when they are touched and that will make noises.

Have a teacher who is trained to work with babies who have vision problems show you how to help your baby learn to get around. Learning to get around is called *mobility training*.

Make sure that your child has safe places to explore (see pages 111-113). Most of the time babies with vision problems like to be rather close to a solid wall or a room divider. It helps them to feel comfortable and safe.

The best basis for your child later learning to read braille or large print is for you to tell your baby stories, teach him finger plays and nursery rhymes, and tell him about the things that are happening.

When people smile and talk to your baby and he doesn't seem to be responding say something like, "Johnny, can you see the pretty lady?" and take the baby close so he might be able to see better. For some people you may need to explain that the baby has trouble seeing, but most people will understand the clue.

There will be times when you feel very badly that your baby is not able to see
the sunset
the parade
or the red of the rose
but don't let him sense those feelings.

Explain the sunset to the baby and allow him to hear the parade and smell the rose.

Your may find that the experiences will sharpen your own vision and appreciation of things.

There are talking books and other services available for the blind from American Council for the Blind, 1211 Connecticut Ave. NW, Washington, DC 20005.

Appendix: Skills Chart

APPENDIX   Skills Chart

Skill Area	Skill Level						
	1 (Infant-6 mo)	2 (Baby-1 yr)	3 (Toddler-2 yr)	4 (Preschool-5 yr)	5 (Elementary-12 yr)	6 (Secondary-18 yr)	7 (Adult-18 yr+)
Motor	Suck Swallow Hold head up Roll over Sit up Crawl	Chew Stand Walk Hold object Throw	Catch Push/pull Climb Run Scribble	Ride tricycle Pull wagon Swim Jump Button Zip Draw with crayons	Draw/write with with pencil Ride bicycle Skate Use scissors Jump rope Play with marbles/ jacks Throw and bat balls Sweep	Typewrite Drive Ski Paint Use basic tools Sew Vacuum Mow lawn	Job skills Design solutions
Language	Eye contact Cry Coo	Babble Combine bab- bling sounds Wave bye-bye Hug	One word utter- ance Play pat-a-cake and peek-a-boo Label objects Request with gesture	Say nursery rhymes Play finger plays Use words about familiar things Speak short sentences Ask and answer *wh* questions Talk about feel- ings	Recite poems Tell stories Recite alphabet Spell Use written lan- guage Read	Compose writing Develop stories Participate in dis- cussions Do library research	Use professional jargon Attend meetings Perform market and social analysis

Social	Recognize parents	Approach family member	Share objects and play area Play beside other children	Play with other children Create games Want to help Interact outside family	Student Sit and rise when told Make friends (own sex)	Maintain friendships Relate to opposite sex Organize group activities	Mating Other partnerships Professional interaction
Self-Help	Cry for help Develop sleep pattern	Coo, babble for help Begin to feed Enjoy bath	Learn to feed self Learn to toilet Undress Learn to wash face and hands Balk at bathing	Dress self with help Feed self with minimal mess Toilet self	Dress alone Begin appropriate food choice Bathe self (difficult areas may be left out) Explore neighborhood alone Learn to pickup after self	Keep personal things/area tidy Purchase own clothes Shampoo self Shower Shave Manage menstruation Manage masturbation Choose appropriate foods Go about town alone	Plan nutrition Select and maintain home and car Travel alone

Handicapping conditions cause difficulty in development. Mildly handicapped children progress more slowly than normally developing children. Severely handicapped children progress even more slowly. They may still be developing Level 5 (elementary - 12 yr) skills when they are chronologically adults. Specific handicapping conditions may make some skills more difficult to acquire than others. Thus, a child may have mastered some skills appropriate for his age in certain areas yet still need work on some lower level skills in other areas. To some extent, however, complete development in each area depends upon development in the other areas. One skill is built upon another. A child must master a skill in Level 1 before he is ready to learn a skill in Level 2. Most children learn skills in the order and approximate ages shown in the Skills Chart.

INDEX

Nursing, *see* Breast feeding

Objects
    baby's unusual use of, 166-168
    learning about through play, 119-120, 122-123, 125-127
Opthalmologist, 17-18
Oral desensitization, 3, 25, 77
Osteogenesis imperfecta, 193
Outdoor play, 124-125
Outings, 110
    in car, 113-114
    to park, 125
    shopping, 72-73
    visiting, 80
Overprotection, 3, 107
Oversensitiveness, as autism, 91-101
    see also Desensitization
Overweight babies, feeding and, 38-39

Parents
    attention of sought by baby, 132-134
    baby in bed of, 45, 134
    friendships of, 80-81
    see also Fathers; Grandparents; Mothers
Park, outdoor play in, 125
Pat-a-cake, learning, 122
PKU (phenylketonuria), 35, 194
Playing
    in bath, 153
    disinterest in, 102-106
    eye problems and, 15
    heart problems and, 184
    hemophilia and, 185
    safety concerns in, 111-114
    toys for, 115-128
    unusual manner of, 160-168
    see also Toys
Play pen, 47
Pneumonia, 12
Pointing, baby's use of, 146-147
Polio, immunization for, 21
Potty chair, for toilet training, 156-162
Preservatives, in diet, 81-82

Rash
    from allergies, 170
    from foods, 7, 35
    from medication, 41
Rectal thermometer, 11
Reflexes
    inhibiting, 71
    uncontrolled movement and, 83-84, 85
Repetition, for learning to talk, 144-145
Rocking, self-stimulation and, 3

Safety, 111-114
    bathing and, 152
    car seats, 114
    "no, no" understood by baby for, 139, 140
    playing and, 121, 124-125
    vision problems and, 197
School program, toilet training and, 161-162
Scoliosis, 92-94, 197
Seizures, 2, 180-181
    falling when sitting and, 75
Self-feeding, 30, 31-32
Self-mutilation, 3
Self-stimulation, 3
    nosebleeds and, 10
Sex organs
    malformations of the, 188
    self-stimulation and, 3
Sharing, toys and, 129-130
Shopping
    baby touching objects while, 127-128
    baby with muscle tone changes and, 72-73
Shoulders, learning to control, 86, 95
Shunt, hydrocephalus and, 186
Siblings, effect of on special baby on, 130, 131
Sickness
    babies frequently having, 10-12
    immunizations and, 21
Side-lying position
    dressing baby in, 163
    hips and shoulders controlled with, 86
    for stiff babies, 60-63, 68
Side-sitting position
    for baby with muscle tone changes, 75
    for stiff babies, 63, 64-65, 68
Sight problems, *see* Eye problems
Sisters, effect of on special baby, 130
Sitting
    baby with muscle tone changes and, 75-76
    eating while, 29-30
    seat with support for, 69, 72
    for stiff babies, 63, 64-68
    turning over and, 86
Skin
    allergies, 170
    bathing and, 152, 154
Sleeping, 44
    away from home, 47
    boredom causing, 50
    in car, 48
    cerebral palsy and, 50
    dependence on mother and, 110
    excessive, 49-51
    lack of desire for, 47-48
    learning when to sleep, 46
    in parents' bed, 45, 134
    restlessness, 46
    routines and, 48-49, 50-51